WYOMING'S
Friendly Skies

Training America's First Stewardesses

STARLEY TALBOTT AND MICHAEL E. KASSEL

Foreword by Patty Kessler and Alda Kessler Stewart

THE
History
PRESS

Published by The History Press
Charleston, SC
www.historypress.com

Often referred to as "The Original Eight," the first graduating class poses in front of a Boeing Model 80A in May 1930 at the Cheyenne, Wyoming airport. *Left to right, top row*: Ellen Church and Alva Johnson; *lower row*: Margaret Arnott, Inez Keller, Cornelia Peterman, Harriet Fry, Jessie Carter and Ellis Crawford. *United Air Lines.*

First published 2020

Manufactured in the United States

ISBN 9781467147637

Library of Congress Control Number: 2020938455

Contents

Foreword   5
Acknowledgements   9
Introduction   11

1. A Sky-High Idea   15
2. Modifications   34
3. Cheyenne's Friendly Skies   56
4. The Early Sky Girls   76
5. Cheyenne's Sky Girl Graduates   89
6. Farewell to an Era   125

Notes   135
Bibliography   141
About the Authors   143

Foreword

The first training event in the world for newly hired airline stewardesses was held in Cheyenne, Wyoming, in 1930. This milestone ranks alongside Devil's Tower and Yellowstone National Park as one of the many national firsts that Wyoming can boast about.

Seasoned authors Starley Talbott and Michael Kassel bring the experience of the thousands of young women who attended flight training school in Cheyenne to life in *Wyoming's Friendly Skies*. Most important to me is one of those graduates, my aunt Alda Kessler Stewart, who trained at United Air Lines Cheyenne facilities and flew those friendly skies for a year in the 1950s. Her natural warmth and charm must have been welcomed by the passengers she served, including actor Jimmy Stewart, who was aboard a United Air Lines charter flight she worked.

My aunt's job aboard planes also came with family perks. During my aunt's tenure as a stewardess with United Air Lines, my grandmother, my aunt's mother, Olive Kessler, accompanied by my father, Charles Kessler, took advantage of a reduced-rate flight for family members of United employees and left the family ranch in southeastern Wyoming for New York City. On their return trip, they flew to Los Angeles, which at that time was Aunt Alda's home base. This transcontinental trip must have been the adventure of a lifetime for my grandmother, who, before that time, had not ventured far from her birthplace and home on Bear Creek in Goshen County, where she had raised my aunt and her seven siblings. This is just one of the many stories of the ways in which the United Stewardess Training

School in Cheyenne affected the lives of individuals in Wyoming. These stories uniquely recommend *Wyoming's Friendly Skies* as a chronicle of the social and economic impact that the early commercial airline industry had in the state.

In a recent conversation, my aunt expressed her delight in her reading of the author's manuscript. Her initial response was, "I just admire these two authors for writing this book. The research was just wonderful." She is right; the research is stellar. The book carefully documents how the requirements and training for the young women attending the stewardess training schools evolved over time, relaxing the strict qualifications for initial apprentices of the flying school, including height and weight requirements. A careful study of the training manuals for these young women over the next thirty years reflects the changing technological innovations in the flight industry as well as those of the role of women in American society. Talbott's and Kassel's book goes beyond recounting the inner workings of a training school for stewardesses. It provides a platform from which graduates of the school, like Aunt Alda who, at the age of ninety-one, continues to fly throughout the world, have been able to share an intimate view of what life was like for these young apprentices during their training and careers as airline stewardesses.

For me, as an instructor of Wyoming history, *Wyoming's Friendly Skies* also opens a fresh dimension to the telling of the story of Wyoming and the central role it played in innovations in the early days of national aviation and passenger flight. Countering the myth of the West and the predominance of Wyoming's image as a cowboy state, the book highlights the role of women shaping the commercial aeronautics industry at a time when Cheyenne seemed poised to become a Great Plains aviation hub. Despite strong initial resistance from pilots, co-pilots and their wives, stewardesses soon gained acceptance and willingly took on roles outside of just assisting passengers, like sometimes refueling planes or cutting down fences when a plane made an unscheduled landing in a farmer's field.

The first training school in Cheyenne in 1930 must have been a welcome boost to the economy. While the rest of the nation was just beginning to feel the effect of the stock market crash of 1929, Wyoming and other states in the region had already been in the midst of a depression throughout most of the 1920s. Midway between flight centers on the Pacific coast and Chicago, Cheyenne was in a unique position to host the early training center for stewardesses and served as a center of activity for the airline industry during World War II. In 1936, a formal training school was later moved east to Chicago. The advent of World War II, however, led to the building of an airline modification center in Cheyenne by United Air Lines. While this once again resulted in growth to Cheyenne's economy (at one point in time, 1,600 people worked from these centers), true to the boom-and-bust nature of Wyoming's economy, following the war, the airline industry took its business south to Denver and farther west to San Francisco. Despite this, rather than leave its once flagship city high and dry, United relocated its formal stewardess training school back to Cheyenne, and it is there that my aunt's brief career with the airline began.

Talbott's and Kassel's book retells the story of the early commercial aviation history, when the interiors of passenger planes were designed to mimic the luxurious trappings of a train coach but were subjected to the conditions inherent in midair flight. The authors tell how the uninsulated cabin was chilly in winter and warm in summer. So the windows slid open or rolled down to provide fresh air for the passengers. The open windows drew engine fumes into the cabin, and the noise from the engines made it nearly impossible to carry on a conversation. These were the conditions that passengers on early flights faced and were the incentive behind the early stewardess training schools. Talbott and Kassel walk the reader through the evolution of a profession custom-designed for women who were interested in a career at a time when few professional opportunities were available to women—a profession that promised an opportunity, in an industry once dominated by men, that young women of the time would not have normally had.

Of particular interest in this book are the personal accounts of the early Sky Girls and Cheyenne's Sky Girl graduates. These oral histories add an intimate dimension to this story and provide an insight into what motivated these individuals to board the midcentury propeller planes and embark on a career that my aunt described as an opportunity "to do something really exciting; for the adventure." My aunt and I invite you to take off with us on this skyward journey into the friendly skies with the courageous and adventurous stewardesses of the United Air Lines Cheyenne training facility.

—Alda Marie Kessler Stewart, Cheyenne Sky Girl graduate;
Patty Kessler, instructor of history and American studies at
Laramie County Community College, Albany County, Wyoming campus

Acknowledgements

The authors are grateful for the many people who made the compilation of this book a reality. Without the courage of the first women who became stewardesses and all those who followed there would be no story, and without the writing, research and assistance of many historians, we could not have written this narrative.

Special thanks go to the staff and volunteers at the Wyoming State Archives, especially Suzi Taylor and Robin Everett. Their ability to locate historical materials is remarkable.

A very special thank-you goes to Barbara Hanson, historical consultant, at United Air Lines Archives in Chicago, Illinois. Her extensive knowledge and care of the collection pertaining to stewardesses was of immense help to us. Barbara kindly spent two days with us as we combed through files and scanned photos and documents. We are also grateful for United Air Lines for allowing us access to its archival collections.

We are grateful to the Wyoming State Historical Society for its role in maintaining Wyoming history. We thank the society for awarding us a Homsher Grant to support our research expenses. We also thank the staff at the American Heritage Center for their assistance. Their efforts to include historical data and artifacts in their extensive collections are extremely valuable.

The efforts of many people who provided information from personal collections are appreciated. We thank Patricia Seibel Romeo and her family for a delightful visit in Denver. We are grateful for information provided by Tom Goodyear, Bonita Ades, Marvin Berryman, Laura Coats, Bonnie Dahl, Marion Hall, Donald LaFarge and Phyllis Jack of the United Airlines Historical Foundation and for hosting us for a visit at the United Airlines Flight Training Center in Denver. We thank Phyllis Jack and Millie Fitzpatrick of Denver for sharing their stewardess memories with us. We also greatly appreciate Alda Kessler Stewart, Patty Kessler, Elvira Call and Barbara Loftus for sharing their information and stories.

Special thanks to our acquisitions editor, Artie Crisp, and others at The History Press for their support and guidance.

Most importantly, we are grateful for our families and our spouses. Michael thanks his wife, Amy, who has been the wind beneath his wings blessing him with her encouragement and fortitude. Starley thanks her husband, Beauford Thompson, for his support in so many ways. Starley thanks her coauthor, Michael Kassel, for his important research on the subject and for his speaking ability, which first inspired her to delve further into the fascinating history about the training of the first stewardesses and others in Cheyenne, Wyoming.

Lastly, we thank our readers and the many people who continue to inspire us with a love of history.

Introduction

Cheyenne's municipal airport played a significant role in the development of early aviation in America. Beginning in 1920, Cheyenne's airport was one of the finest in the nation and served as a main stop on the first transcontinental airmail route. The airfield was the original home of Boeing Air Transport. It also served as an airplane modification center during World War II and the base for the United Air Lines Stewardess Training facility for several years.

Boeing Air Transport Company operated in Cheyenne and was contracted to operate the airmail service in 1927. It also began providing passenger service, although carrying the mail was still a priority. Boeing Air Transport eventually combined with Pacific Air Transport, National Air Transport and Varney Airlines to form United Air Lines in 1934.

By 1930, Steve Stimpson, manager of the Boeing Air Transport Company's Pacific Division in the San Francisco office, had become concerned about the need for caring for passengers on flights. All airlines were having difficulties encouraging the public to fly, as most had experienced airplanes as good only for war or for barnstorming. Stimpson had previously worked for a steamship line and noticed how the ship's stewards helped the passengers. Other airlines had come to this conclusion as well and employed men as stewards prior to 1930. Stimpson sought a solution that would solve both problems of promoting air travel and caring for passengers at the same time.

The solutions came from an unexpected direction. Ellen Church, a young registered nurse living in San Francisco, often passed by the office of Boeing company on her way to work at the French Hospital. One day, she entered the office and asked Stimpson if she could get a job on an airplane. He was not able to offer her a job, but as they conversed during future visits, they agreed that women might be able to assist with the problem of taking care of airline passengers. Stimpson eventually presented the idea of hiring women to officials at Boeing and was given permission to hire the world's first stewardesses.

Management was skeptical at first but decided to try the addition of young women as part of the flight crew. The presence of warm, knowledgeable and professional women might be a strong factor to convince the public to fly.

Eight candidates applied to be the first stewardesses and were flown to Cheyenne in May 1930 to receive training. The experience was planned for four days but lasted for two weeks when the group became snowbound. Following the course in Cheyenne, the eight young women went their separate ways.

Cheyenne was the halfway point of the San Francisco to Chicago route being operated by Boeing Air Transport. Four of the original stewardesses worked the San Francisco to Cheyenne leg of the flight, and four traveled between Cheyenne and Chicago. Their duties were numerous and varied, including cleaning the cabin, aiding passengers to board, serving food and comforting passengers.

Originally, pilots and crews wanted little to do with the new stewardesses. However, these eight women, followed by hundreds of others, soon proved their worth to the crews, passengers and the public at large by working hard, being unflappable in difficult circumstances and doing their utmost to make flying a pleasant experience. The tenure of the first eight stewardesses created a career and a legacy that has become an institution in commercial flying. By the end of the decade, the stewardess had become an indispensable part of the airline industry.

Stewardesses in Cheyenne continued to be trained in rather informal settings, often by the stewardesses who preceded each new group of women. United Air Lines opened a stewardess school in Chicago in 1936, and other airlines established training facilities elsewhere.

Commercial aviation was important to the Cheyenne airport during the 1940s. The advent of World War II offered a boon to the economy of the city. In support of the war effort, the United Air Lines maintenance facility was expanded to become the Cheyenne Modification Center. The facility employed hundreds of people and was responsible for the upgrade of thousands of B-17 bombers for the war in Europe. During the war, many of the stewardess nurses became military nurses, resulting in a shortage of trained airline attendants. United had also moved its flight training division from California to Cheyenne. Operations in the city ran continuously until the end of the war, when many of the airline-related industries abandoned Cheyenne.

United Air Lines expanded its routes in 1947 by inaugurating flights to Hawaii, made possible by the large and powerful DC-6 aircraft. After the introduction of the DC-6, Cheyenne's maintenance facility was moved to San Francisco to a new center that was specifically tailored for the advanced aircraft. The flight training program was moved to Denver.

Following the loss of hundreds of jobs related to the airline industry, United offered to relocate its stewardess school to Cheyenne. The company recognized the value of the long-term relationship with the city and decided not to abandon it completely. The stewardess training center in Chicago had been demolished to provide space for more hangars, thus making it necessary to find new quarters for the school.

United Air Lines opened a formal stewardess training school in Cheyenne in 1947. The new facility was located in the building that had formerly housed the modification center, thus saving the company money by not having to build a new structure. The facility was housed in the office addition to the west of hangar number three, utilizing all three floors of that building. The cafeteria was located in a building between hangars two and three, and a mockup of an airplane was located in one of the hangars.

Some young women who arrived in Cheyenne to attend the stewardess school were undoubtedly shocked when they learned they would be housed in a dormitory, sharing space with their classmates. Others complained that the area was in the middle of nowhere. Most of them adjusted to the conditions, made friends and even came to enjoy Cheyenne. During their leisure time, they often frequented local restaurants and bars. Favorite places to meet included the Belecky Ranch, the Little Bear Inn and the Wigwam Lounge in the Plains Hotel.

During the school's years of service in Cheyenne, more than six thousand stewardesses completed their education. With the arrival of the jet age in 1958, educational needs began to change. To meet the demands of commercial jet travel, United Air Lines constructed a new training school at Chicago, closing the Cheyenne facility in 1961.

With the closing of the stewardess school, Cheyenne lost its last direct connection to an airline that had been a strong economic partner since the late 1920s. The November 2, 1961 edition of the *Wyoming Eagle* lamented that aside from the loss of the economic benefits of the stewardess school, the city also lost a romantic connection to a time when ladies of the sky visited the Wigwam Lounge. The town and its airfield became quieter in 1961 with the loss of the school, and several people yearned for the time when Wyoming gave the ambassadors of the "Friendly Skies" their wings.

1

A Sky-High Idea

A woman walked into a man's California office in 1930 and changed the culture of the male-dominated aviation industry. A young nurse named Ellen wanted to fly home to Iowa for a visit, and she dreamed of becoming an airplane pilot.

Ellen Church often passed by the office of the Boeing Air Transport Company's Pacific Division on her way to her job as a registered nurse at the French Hospital in San Francisco. When she stopped in on a spring day in 1930, she met with Steve Stimpson, manager of the office, and told him she was interested in obtaining a flying job and possibly becoming an airline pilot.

Stimpson was not able to offer her a job in the airline industry since flying was an exclusively male occupation. Even so, Church often returned to the office to visit, and they became friends.

Eventually, the conversations moved in the direction of how Stimpson's airline was struggling to get a profitable number of passengers. People, it seemed, saw air travel as the realm of airmail pilots and barnstormers, not a safe and reliable mode of travel. In Stimpson's mind, one of the aspects that contributed to the rough popular perception of the new industry was the primitive state of service it offered, and something had to be done. Even the best minds in the industry were struggling to come up with a solution.[1]

The company that Stimpson worked for, Boeing Air Transport, was the brainchild of legendary aviation designer and entrepreneur William Boeing. The idea originated with the passage of the Kelly Air Mail Act in

Left: Ellen Church worked at the French Hospital in San Francisco before becoming the world's first airline stewardess in 1930. *United Air Lines.*

Right: Steve Stimpson was the manager of the Boeing Air Transport Pacific division in San Francisco. *United Air Lines.*

1926, which removed the government from the business of carrying the mails through the nation's skies. The intent was to pass the responsibility to private companies that could do it more efficiently. Boeing knew that he could improve the service immediately by designing new aircraft that were superior in every way to the World War I–vintage machines then operated by the U.S. Air Mail Service. There was a twist, however, that challenged even Boeing's vaunted skills. The Kelly Air Mail Act demanded that private companies carry not only mail but paying passengers as well. To do this, Boeing designed his first attempt to meet this requirement, the unprecedented Boeing 40-A. Like all planes that carried the mail before, the craft was a biplane in which the pilot sat in a cockpit exposed to the elements, as was the preference at the time. What set this plane apart was that a small compartment was added in front of the pilot to house four passengers inside the cramped fuselage right behind the engine. The only amenities offered were chairs and a window on either side that allowed the sardine-packed souls to see the countryside glide below them. If they had any needs during the journey, they were on their own, as there was no way for the pilot to communicate with them or assist in any way. Fortunately, the duration between stops was small. Boeing realized that this was no way to develop a winning passenger business.[2]

Boeing's next aircraft was the significantly larger Boeing 80-A. Monstrous in comparison, it was Boeing's first true airliner. The plane had three engines, and the pilot was joined by a co-pilot in an enclosed cockpit. Behind them was a lavishly appointed cabin for the passengers.

The Boeing Aircraft 80-A had a capacity for twelve passengers and the mail. The interior of the cabin was designed to resemble a train coach, often referred to as a Flying Pullman, to reassure passengers by putting them in a familiar setting. The cabin was wood paneled with wide square windows for viewing during the day and elegant lighting fixtures for lighting at night. The passengers were comfortably seated in wicker chairs bolted to the floor. However, the uninsulated cabin was chilly in winter and warm in summer, so the windows were slid open or rolled down to provide fresh air for the passengers. The open windows drew engine fumes into the cabin, and the noise from the engines made it nearly impossible to carry on a conversation. Most planes had toilet facilities, including a small sink and hot and cold running water, but the toilet itself was simply a seat that opened to reveal a hole in the floor.[3]

The comfort for the flying guests of the company was far better but still needed improvement. Stimpson recalled his experiences while traveling on company business with these words:

> Back in those days it was the co-pilot's job to look after the passengers. He passed out box lunches and served coffee from a thermos bottle. He'd often get his thumb in the coffee. If the passengers got airsick, which they often did in those little upsy-daisy planes, he also gave them sympathy, if he had time, which wasn't often.
>
> I traveled by plane on business as it was my job to open new offices as business increased. It was obvious to me that the co-pilot needed some help in caring for the passengers, especially when the flying was rough. The planes flew at about one hundred miles per hour, barely fast enough to stay in the air, so we couldn't fly very high. Consequently, rough flights were the usual thing, and passengers often got airsick. When I was aboard, I was glad to help take care of the passengers, as the co-pilot usually had something more important to do.[4]

Beginning in 1930, Boeing Air Transport stewardesses trained in the Boeing Model 80A, a three-engine biplane that could carry up to twelve passengers. *Starley Talbott collection.*

The situation for passengers still wasn't a great selling point, but Stimpson had an idea and he shared this with Ellen Church. He had been working on the concept of hiring young men to be stewards on an airplane, much as they served as stewards on steamships.

After World War I, Stimpson completed his duties with the army and hired on with a steamship line. He was interested in aviation, however, and took a job with Boeing Air Transport in San Francisco. While working for the steamship line, Stimpson had noticed how the ship's stewards helped the passengers, so he thought that perhaps stewards could be hired for the airlines. A few male stewards were employed by other airlines prior to 1930.[5]

While discussing the possibility of hiring stewards to attend to passengers on an airline during one of Ellen Church's visits to Stimpson's office, she countered with her own proposal:

> *Why not stewardesses, girls who are registered nurses. The psychology of girls aboard your planes, and registered nurses, too, would sell more tickets than all the traffic representatives you could hire. Nurses would be able to look after passengers and assure them that the flight would be safe.*[6]

The vision to have nurses become the first airline stewardesses struck Stimpson as a logical choice, and he agreed with Church. Nurses would be able to help passengers who became ill, would be sensitive to individual needs and have a strong empathy with the passengers. He thought that the addition of young women as part of the flight crew would allay the concerns of the public. The presence of warm, knowledgeable and professional women would be a strong factor in convincing the public to fly.

Stimpson wrote the following correspondence in 1930 promoting the idea of stewardess service to W.A. Patterson. Patterson was known as "Big Pat" and was the manager of the Cheyenne, Wyoming office of Boeing Air Transport.

As a suggestion—I was just wondering if you had ever given any serious thought to the subject of young women as couriers. It strikes me that there would be a great psychological punch to having young women stewardesses or couriers, or whatever you want to call them, and I am certain that there are some mighty good ones available. I have in mind a couple of graduate nurses that would make exceptional stewardesses. Of course it would be distinctly understood that there would be no reference made to their hospital training or nursing experience, but it would be a mighty fine thing to have this available if necessary either for air sickness or something else worse.

Imagine the psychology of having young women as regular members of the crew. Imagine the national publicity we could get from it, and the tremendous effect it would have on the traveling public. Also imagine the value that they would be to us not only in the neater and nicer method of serving food and looking out for the passenger's welfare, but also in an emergency.

I am not suggesting at all the flapper type of girl, or one that would go haywire. You know nurses as well as I do, and you know that they are not given to flightiness—I mean in the head. The average graduate nurse is a girl with some horse sense and is very practical and has seen enough of men to not be inclined to chase them around the block at every opportunity. Further, as a general rule nurses are not of the "pretty" type which lends to their usefulness in this case.

The young women that we would select would naturally be intelligent and could handle what traffic work aboard was necessary, such as keeping of records, filling out reports, issuing tickets, etc., etc. They would probably do this as well or better than the average young fellow. Further, while we admit to ourselves that we are going to train couriers for ultimate jobs ashore in various traffic capacities, we know between ourselves that there is anything but a dearth of opportunities in sight.

As to the qualifications of the proposed young women couriers, their first paramount qualification would be that of a graduate nurse (although this would never be brought in the foreground in advertising or anything as it sort of sounds as though they are necessary); and, secondly, young women who have been around and are familiar with general travel, rail, steamer and air. Such young women are available here.

This is just a passing thought and I want to pass it on to you.[7]

DOMESTIC SERVICE
Check the class of service desired;
otherwise this message will be
sent as a full rate telegram

| FULL RATE TELEGRAM | SERIAL |
| DAY LETTER | NIGHT LETTER |

WESTERN UNION

W. P. MARSHALL, PRESIDENT

1211

INTERNATIONAL SERVICE
Check the class of service desired;
otherwise this message will be
sent at the full rate

| FULL RATE | DEFERRED |
| CODE | NIGHT LETTER |

| NO. WDS.-CL. OF SVC. | PD. OR COLL. | CASH NO. | CHARGE TO THE ACCOUNT OF | TIME FILED |

Send the following message, subject to the terms on back hereof, which are hereby agreed to

TO: W. A. PATTERSON, ASSISTANT TO PRESIDENT   SAN FRANCISCO, CALIFORNIA
    UNITED AIR LINES, INC.   FEBRUARY 24, 1930
    SEATTLE, WASHINGTON

AS A SUGGESTION — I WAS JUST WONDERING IF YOU HAD EVER GIVEN ANY SERIOUS THOUGHT TO THE
SUBJECT OF YOUNG WOMEN AS COURIERS. IT STRIKES ME THAT THERE WOULD BE A GREAT PSYCHOLO-
GICAL PUNCH TO HAVING YOUNG WOMEN STEWARDESSES OR COURIERS, OR WHATEVER YOU WANT TO CALL
THEM, AND I AM CERTAIN THAT THERE ARE SOME MIGHTY GOOD ONES AVAILABLE. I HAVE IN MIND A
COUPLE OF GRADUATE NURSES WHO WOULD MAKE EXCEPTIONAL STEWARDESSES. OF COURSE IT WOULD
BE DISTINCTLY UNDERSTOOD THAT THERE WOULD BE NO REFERENCE MADE TO THEIR HOSPITAL TRAINING
OR NURSING EXPERIENCE, BUT IT WOULD BE A MIGHTY FINE THING TO HAVE THIS AVAILABLE, SUB ROSA,
IF NECESSARY FOR AIR SICKNESS.

IMAGINE THE PSYCHOLOGY OF HAVING YOUNG WOMEN AS REGULAR MEMBERS OF THE CREW: IMAGINE
THE NATIONAL PUBLICITY WE COULD GET FROM IT, AND THE TREMENDOUS EFFECT IT WOULD HAVE ON
THE TRAVELING PUBLIC. ALSO IMAGINE THE VALUE THAT THEY WOULD BE TO US IN THE NEATER AND
NICER METHOD OF SERVING FOOD AND LOOKING OUT FOR THE PASSENGERS' WELFARE.

I AM NOT SUGGESTING AT ALL THE FLAPPER TYPE OF GIRL. YOU KNOW NURSES AS WELL AS I DO, AND
YOU KNOW THAT THEY ARE NOT GIVEN TO FLIGHTINESS. THE AVERAGE GRADUATE NURSE IS A GIRL
WITH SOME HORSE SENSE AND IS VERY PRACTICAL AND HAS SEEN ENOUGH OF MEN TO NOT BE INCLINED
TO CHASE THEM AROUND THE BLOCK AT EVERY OPPORTUNITY. FURTHER, AS A GENERAL RULE NURSES
ARE NOT OF THE "PRETTY" TYPE WHICH LENDS TO THEIR USEFULNESS IN THIS CASE.

THE YOUNG WOMEN WHOM WE WOULD SELECT WOULD NATURALLY BE INTELLIGENT AND COULD HANDLE WHAT
TRAFFIC WORK ABOARD WAS NECESSARY, SUCH AS THE KEEPING OF RECORDS, FILLING OUT REPORTS,
ISSUING TICKETS, ETC. ETC. THEY WOULD PROBABLY DO THIS AS WELL OR BETTER THAN THE AVERAGE
YOUNG FELLOW. FURTHER, WHILE WE ADMIT TO OURSELVES THAT WE ARE GOING TO TRAIN COURIERS
FOR ULTIMATE JOBS ASHORE IN VARIOUS TRAFFIC CAPACITIES, WE KNOW BETWEEN OURSELVES THAT
THERE IS ANYTHING BUT A DEARTH OF OPPORTUNITIES IN SIGHT.

AS TO THE QUALIFICATIONS OF THE PROPOSED YOUNG WOMEN COURIERS, THEIR FIRST PARAMOUNT
QUALIFICATION WOULD BE THAT OF A GRADUATE NURSE (ALTHOUGH THIS WOULD NEVER BE BROUGHT IN-
TO THE FOREGROUND IN ADVERTISING OR ANYTHING AS IT SORT OF SOUNDS AS THOUGH THEY ARE
NECESSARY); AND, SECONDLY, YOUNG WOMEN WHO HAVE BEEN AROUND AND ARE FAMILIAR WITH GENERAL
TRAVEL, - RAIL, STEAMER AND AIR. SUCH YOUNG WOMEN ARE AVAILABLE HERE.

THIS IS JUST A PASSING THOUGHT.

                                        S. A. STIMPSON
                                        DIVISION TRAFFIC AGENT

Steve Stimpson sent this message to both William "Big Pat" Patterson at the Cheyenne, Wyoming airport and to William "Little Pat" Patterson, assistant director of Boeing Air Transport, suggesting the idea of hiring women as stewardesses. *United Air Lines.*

Back came the succinct reply from Big Pat Patterson, the manager at the Cheyenne airport: No.[8]

Undaunted, Stimpson promptly sent off the same request to another W.A. Patterson (known as "Little Pat"), then the assistant director of Boeing Air Transport. Patterson was skeptical, too, but he asked his wife, Vera, what

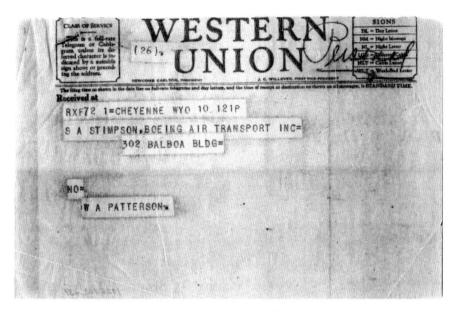

William "Big Pat" Patterson, who was employed at the Cheyenne airport, sent this succinct reply to Steve Stimpson. He resigned soon after rejecting Stimpson's idea. *United Air Lines.*

she thought of the idea. Vera Patterson thought it was a good idea, so her husband agreed and told Stimpson he could begin his stewardess program on a three-month trial basis. Other executives were still opposed, and one stated, "If Boeing Air Transport is going to set up a circus performance, consider this my resignation." Patterson wired back: "Your resignation is accepted." Soon after, "Big Pat" of the Cheyenne office also resigned.[9]

In collaboration with Ellen Church, Stimpson began a search for suitable candidates for stewardess training. He soon found that not so many registered nurses were anxious to leave their current positions for an unknown career at an airline. Stimpson jokingly told friends he had been ejected from every hospital in San Francisco when he showed up looking for nurse recruits. He eventually hired four candidates from the San Francisco area, including Ellen Church.[10]

It was decided to recruit four candidates from San Francisco and four candidates from Chicago and have the new recruits travel to Cheyenne, Wyoming, for training. Ellen Church interviewed a number of nurses in Chicago and hired four of them. Some of these young women and their parents were also skeptical of the role their daughters would play. When one of the new hires, Jessie Carter, told her parents she was flying to Cheyenne to learn about her new job, they thought she said she was going to China.

It was reported that Carter's parents were not as alarmed about her flying halfway around the world as they were about their daughter flying anywhere, unescorted, with men.[11]

Qualifications for the beginning group of stewardesses were strict. Requirements stated the candidate must be a graduate nurse, unmarried, no older than twenty-five, no taller than five feet, four inches and no more than 115 pounds. The height and weight requirements were practical considerations because the aircraft of the time were tiny by modern standards. The planes had narrow aisles and low ceilings, making movement inside them difficult. Because the aircraft had small engines, the weight of the crew, passengers and luggage had a significant effect on the plane's performance and therefore safety.[12]

The original group of stewardesses had included one married woman, Ellis Crawford. Her husband called Stimpson day and night to find out when his wife would be home, and Stimpson decided that business didn't mix very well with marriage. He added the stipulation that all candidates must be unmarried.[13]

With the candidates in hand, the effort moved to the small high-plains city of Cheyenne, Wyoming, situated almost directly halfway between Chicago and San Francisco. The choice of sending the prospective stewardesses to the small Wyoming capital for training wasn't a fluke. Cheyenne served as Boeing Air Transport's national headquarters and boasted one of the finest airfields in the nation. More importantly, it served as the main maintenance depot, training and administrative center for the young airline.[14]

Finally, the new recruits gathered in Cheyenne, Wyoming, in mid-May 1930 for training. A United Air Lines historical document noted, "When they reached Cheyenne all eight of the girls were snowbound for two weeks at the Plains Hotel and ate up $300 worth of food—all this before they had even gone into service."[15]

Their appearance coincided with even greater numbers of the Boeing aircraft coming into service at the city. This did not go unnoticed. The May 14, 1930 edition of the *Wyoming Tribune* stated:

> *Cheyenne's star is in the ascendant. One good thing seems to lead to another. The advent of the new tri-motor 16-passenger planes has aroused new interest locally and increased traffic between San Francisco and Chicago. The latest innovation is the arrival in Cheyenne of eight beautiful young women, gowned in uniforms of gray-green. Their presence at the Plains Hotel has attracted much favorable comment and curiosity. Each girl is*

selected for a high degree of intelligence, and all of them are graduate nurses from accredited hospitals in San Francisco and Chicago. A special suite of rooms is maintained for them in the Plains Hotel in Cheyenne.[16]

According to Steve Stimpson, the training sessions for the new stewardesses included lectures and discussions of their tasks. Stimpson wrote the first stewardess manual, a pamphlet of four pages. The foreword to the manual stated:

> The Boeing System, from the inception of its passenger service, has striven to maintain the highest possible standard of cuisine and service to its passengers. In desiring to accomplish this, we are issuing this general circular, with supplements as may be necessary, in order to keep you informed in the most concise manner possible as to our ideas of what this high standard should consist of.
>
> It does not mean that you are not to use your own initiative in perfecting your duties to the highest possible extent: we are merely trying to point out the minimum which we consider necessary.
>
> This circular, together with supplements, must be considered a permanent record and kept carefully by each young woman in her possessions aboard plane for ready reference. Upon changing personnel, it should be turned over to the Chief Stewardess, and receipt taken therefor.
>
> We shall be very pleased at all times to receive constructive criticisms or suggestions you may have regarding our service, as we are constantly striving to have the Boeing System represent the very highest standards of air transportation.
>
> The stewardesses are the only representative of the Traffic Department aboard the planes, and the Traffic Department's chief and principal function is that of contact between the public and the Boeing System for the purpose of increasing traffic. Service must be rendered to increase traffic, and we must go out of our way at all times to be extraordinarily polite and perform each and every duty in an obliging manner for the passenger.[17]

The duties included tagging passenger baggage and loading it aboard; punching each ticket at each point on the route; seeing to it that planes were property heated and ventilated; and carrying aboard hampers filled with cold chicken, apples, rolls, cake, and vacuum bottles of hot beverages.

Additional directions stipulated: keep the cabin immaculate; before each flight, sweep the floor and dust off the seats and windowsills; check the floor bolts and make sure that all seats are securely fastened to the floor; keep the clock and altimeter wound up; correct the time as the aircraft passes through time zones; keep an eye on passengers when they go to the toilet room to be sure they go through the toilet room door and not through the emergency exit door; warn passengers against throwing anything out the window; and carry a railroad time table just in case the plane is grounded somewhere. They also handed out blankets for passengers to stay warm on drafty airplanes. They often found themselves helping to fuel the airplane, as well.

Stewardesses were also reminded to care for the passengers in many ways, including these suggestions:

> Some of our passengers may appear very retiring and without wants and it is up to the stewardess to occasionally make inquiries if they can be of service. A passenger may want a pillow or a chair adjusted, or a blanket, or a glass of cold water, or a magazine might be required. This sometimes cannot be determined without our asking. A passenger might feel slightly air sick and be hesitant about giving notice. It is much better to be on the alert and offer to escort the passengers to the washroom, or in an emergency offer the waxed cups that are aboard for this purpose, rather than to run the risk of getting the plane soiled. Right here we might add that a soiled plane is extremely uninviting and quite impossible to clean up very well until the next stop. The cleanliness of the cabins is extremely important at all times; nothing will turn the stomachs of others quicker than an untidy cabin.[18]

Ellen Church was named the chief stewardess and participated in planning and conducting the training. She and Stimpson designed the distinctive new uniforms: a dark green double-breasted jacket and skirt with a green tam shaped like a shower cap and a flowing green cape with a gray collar and silver buttons. The cape had large enough pockets to hold a wrench, a screwdriver and a railroad timetable, useful items each stewardess would need to carry out her duties. The colors of the uniform were significant because they were the colors of the Boeing Air Transport planes. Each stewardess was also issued a second uniform of a light gray smock and light gray nurse's cap to be worn while serving passengers aboard the aircraft.[19]

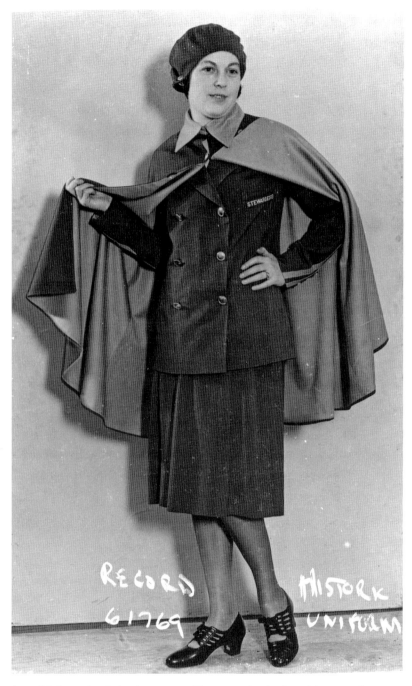

A model shows the distinctive green uniform worn by the first eight stewardesses beginning in 1930. *United Air Lines.*

The training manual described the new uniforms and their care along with the procedure for wearing the uniform:

> The best personal care should be taken of these uniforms, and they should be kept neat, clean and pressed at all times. The field uniform is to be worn to and from the fields at home ports around our hangars, and also while at Cheyenne or other intermediate lay-overs. It is to be worn aboard planes while leaving from each home port, and while taking off, and stewardesses will shortly thereafter change to the cabin uniform consisting of the grey smock and nurse's cap. The grey smock can either be worn over the green uniform, or by taking off the uniform jacket, according to temperature. Then again, if it is quite chilly, the stewardess can slip the cape on over the cabin uniform while resting and to keep her comfortable. Care should be taken to carefully hang up the field uniform in the cabin aboard the planes while not in use. Field uniform should be changed into before arriving at the final destination.[20]

When the stewardesses received their new uniforms, they were photographed together at the door of a Boeing Air Transport plane in Cheyenne and in the reception area of the airport. Soon after, they each went their separate ways on their scheduled routes and were never together at the same time again.

Eight brave women had arrived on the windswept prairies of southeastern Wyoming to embark on an unknown experiment within aviation. Ellen Church, Jessie Carter, Ellis Crawford and Inez Keller would fly the San Francisco to Cheyenne route with stops in Oakland, Sacramento, Reno, Elko, Salt Lake City and Rock Springs. Margaret Arnott, Harriet Fry, Alva Johnson and Cornelia Peterman would fly the Cheyenne to Chicago route with stops in North Platte, Lincoln, Omaha, Des Moines, Cedar Rapids and Iowa City. All of these stops were necessary because carrying the mail was still the most important function of the Boeing Air Transport business. For their work, the new stewardesses would receive a salary of $125 per month for one hundred hours of flying.

As the women began their work for the airline, there were still components from the stewardess manual that needed to be attended to, such as food service:

> We have specially made individual hampers for each plane that will contain all food, dishes, coffee cups, etc. for complete service

The original eight stewardesses pose in front of a Boeing Air Transport Model 80-A after completing training in Cheyenne, Wyoming, in May 1930. *Left to right, top row*: Jessie Carter, Ellis Crawford and Ellen Church; *bottom row*: Inez Keller, Alva Johnson, Harriet Fry, Margaret Arnott and Cornelia Peterman. *United Air Lines.*

An unidentified stewardess serves food to passengers on an early Boeing Air Transport plane. The trimotor plane was modeled to resemble a railroad passenger car and had wicker seats bolted to the floor. *United Air Lines.*

aboard....The greatest care must be exercised in serving of meals aboard, and it must be done very tactfully and daintily. Only cold meals will be served aboard, with hot coffee. A definite time will later be fixed for luncheon hours, but stewardesses' own discretion can be used for the present. Dishes and all food must later be put back in hampers and nothing at all left out around cabin. The specially prepared fruit cocktail will be served as the first course, preceding the sandwiches and/or cold meat.[21]

Hot meals were provided when planes landed in Cheyenne, as explained in the manual:

It is much closer between Chicago and San Francisco than one first imagines via air miles, with result that really only one good hot meal is required. This will be served in our own private dining room at Cheyenne for all passengers, whether east or west bound. In other words, east bound passengers from San Francisco would have a hot breakfast in Cheyenne the next morning, and west bound passengers from Chicago would have a hot dinner at Cheyenne that same night. Be sure that this point is explained to the passengers.[22]

While on duty, stewardesses were allowed expenses, as stipulated in the manual:

Certain expenses for meals and hotel accommodations will be allowed young women on both divisions when away from their respective home ports such as while in Cheyenne or some other intermediate point. No expenses for meals, quarters or transportation will be allowed at home ports. The schedule will indicate that two young women are supposed to be in Cheyenne each night when planes are on time, and for this purpose a permanent room will be kept in the best hotel with twin beds for that purpose. Expenses for meals will be allowed while at Cheyenne.[23]

Other information to be imparted to passengers was described in the manual:

Stewardesses are expected to familiarize themselves as much as possible concerning general subjects of interest to the passengers. Lights and objects below while in flight are of interest to passengers, and special pains must be taken to identify all this as much as possible for the information and entertainment of passengers.

Passengers should be talked to when they so desire, but it is not recommended that conversations be prompted on our part, as conversation aboard is sometimes not so desirable. Be sure to answer any questions, however, in a diplomatic manner, but no guessing should be done concerning matters with which you are not familiar. Many questions will be asked, such as speed of plane, altitude, horse power, gasoline consumption, next stop, price of planes, if not why, etc. etc., so just as soon as possible stewardesses must familiarize themselves with the general subjects. It is recommended that names of passengers be learned as soon as possible, either from ticket or in some other manner, as this is a little touch of personal service that is appreciated by all passengers.

Remember at all times when on duty to retain the respectful reserve of the well-trained servant. A ready smile is essential, but never permit yourself the intimate attitude of a travelling companion.

Face the rear of the cabin when talking with passengers or serving lunch. Bending over while facing toward the front of the plane tends to place the seat of your pants in the passenger's face. Tuck your skirt in carefully and assume a lady-like squatting position beside the passenger when carrying on a conversation.

When slippers are available on long night flights you will advise persons desiring to sleep as follows, "I have slippers available, sir, if you would care to remove your shoes and rest your feet." Assist the passenger to remove his shoes, if he so desires. Clean the shoes thoroughly before returning them to him. So as not to startle a passenger when awakening him, touch him gently on the shoulder and if this does not work tweak his elbow sharply, that is guaranteed to waken him.[24]

At first the pilots and co-pilots strongly objected to the stewardesses. Steve Stimpson said the pilots were leather-jacketed, two-fisted he-men who considered flying strictly a man's game. They wore guns to protect the mail and didn't want any women around to detract from their masculine importance. The pilots soon changed their minds when they found out the girls were nice to have around and helpful, too. Stewardesses were sometimes called on to help cut down fences if there was a forced landing in a field, and they often helped refuel planes and push aircraft into a hangar.[25]

The wives of some of the pilots began a letter-writing campaign to complain about the stewardesses to Boeing Air Transport. They said the stewardesses were trying to steal their husbands and requested their removal.[26]

By the end of the three-month trial period, the pilots and co-pilots were enthusiastic about the service of stewardesses. Business had also begun to increase, with a large part due to more women passengers. Women seemed to believe that if young girls were willing to work on aircraft, flying couldn't really be dangerous.

Steve Stimpson praised the work of the stewardesses when he reminisced about their service at the Twenty-Fifth Anniversary Stewardess Luncheon at the Ambassador Hotel in Los Angeles on May 12, 1955. He said the stewardesses worked very hard and made many friends for United Air Lines. He related that he received a phone call from a man asking who the crew would be on the eastbound trip the following night. "I checked up, called back and told him the names of the pilot and co-pilot. The passenger got mad and said, 'I don't mean them, who the heck is the girl?'"[27]

Stimpson related another anecdote during his speech at the anniversary luncheon:

> Our new service called for a schedule of twenty hours, San Francisco to Chicago, and we were justly proud of it. This was not as long as it sounds when you consider the stops we made en route: Oakland, Sacramento, Reno, Elko, Salt Lake City, Rock Springs, Cheyenne, North Platte, Lincoln, Omaha, Des Moines, Cedar Rapids, Iowa City and Chicago. The girls wore neat, stiffly starched gray smocks on board, but were required to change into their green uniforms before landing at principal terminals. The situation did occur when we had tail winds blowing us across the country and into airports ahead of schedule. In consequence, we found that our girls spent about half their time dressing and undressing.[28]

According to a report in the October 1930 *Boeing News*, passengers were appreciative of the services provided by staff on board the planes. The Chicago office received the following note:

> After having travelled about 15,000 miles on your planes I feel that I should be lacking in courtesy if I did not write to you and express my appreciation of the many kindnesses and courtesies received from the personnel of the United Air Lines whilst making my trips. Without exception your pilots

At the thirtieth anniversary of the United Air Lines stewardess service, Ellen Church and Steve Stimpson, the duo who initiated the idea of hiring stewardesses as part of a flight crew, admire a photo of the original eight stewardesses who were trained at Cheyenne, Wyoming, in 1930. *United Air Lines.*

are men of the highest caliber who undoubtedly by their personality give your passengers a feeling of safety and confidence. The stewardesses on the planes are the last word in courtesy and consideration and from the whole of the organization with which I came into contact, including your office and ground crews, I have nothing but the highest admiration.[29]

The October 1931 edition of *United Air Lines News* stated: "The Company has received numerous letters commending certain members of the stewardess staff for the interest they have taken in the passengers, especially when ships have been grounded due to weather."

Being grounded due to weather conditions was a common occurrence in the early days of passenger service. Lysle Wood of the engineering department station in Cheyenne remarked, "Cheyenne wind is annoying. We use a logging chain for a wind sock. When it stands out straight flying goes on as usual, but when the links start snapping off it is customary to keep the ships inside the hangar."[30]

A passenger wrote to *United Air Lines News* in March 1933:

I wish to commend Pilot Thompson, Mate Fisk and Stewardess Jorgensen for the skill and speed with which they handled ship and passengers, looking to their safety and comfort under very trying circumstances, including the landing of the ship at the base of Elk Mountain, Wyoming, in a heavy snow storm, making a perfect landing in an open field along the edge of a deep ravine, followed by a fine takeoff when the storm had cleared. A hot, impromptu meal served at a summer hotel, only the kitchen of which was still open and which at once, under Stewardess Jorgensen's direction got in operation to serve United Air Lines passengers.[31]

The stewardesses had quickly gained the confidence of the flying public. Their dedication and spirit of cooperation rapidly won them a permanent place in what had been a man's domain. Carefully selected and highly trained, they became a vibrant symbol of Steve Stimpson's dream and Ellen Church's courage as they provided the feminine touch and a bright new career for women.

2

Modifications

T he new career acquired for women and put into action by eight brave women in 1930 continued to evolve along with technological advances in the field of aviation. Stewardess training was somewhat informal for several years, with each new group of women trained by the previous group of stewardesses.

Modifications were recorded in the updated stewardess manual of 1931 with some of these details:

REMARKS

The Stewardess Service has been in effect, transcontinental, on the Boeing System going on ten months now, and we have all learned a good deal. There are short-comings as there are in any new undertaking, but we are endeavoring to minimize these and must have the full cooperation and, above all, the strict obedience of all concerned. It was for this reason that we chose professionally trained young women, the type of person accustomed to discipline, as strict discipline is paramount with us at all times.

By the use of young ladies aboard our planes a certain atmosphere and charm is attained that would be lost otherwise, and it is this atmosphere that we want maintained aboard in a friendly but dignified manner at all times.

On a windy day in 1930s Cheyenne, Wyoming, newly recruited Boeing Air Transport stewardesses line up to board a flight on a Boeing Model 80A aircraft. *Wyoming State Archives, Department of State Parks and Cultural Resources.*

NAME OF SERVICE

The name of service still remains Stewardess Service, and the girls, Stewardesses, for want of more appropriate title. Some day one may show up and suggestions are invited.

CHIEF STEWARDESS

The Chief Stewardess maintains direct supervision over the service with headquarters at Cheyenne. The Chief Stewardess must have the full cooperation and complete observance of all instructions. The Chief Stewardess reports, in turn, to the Traffic Department, under which this service directly comes.

DUTIES

The stewardesses are the only representatives of the Traffic Department in contact with the passengers from the time of passenger's embarkation to debarkation, and as one of the prime functions of the Traffic Department is contact with the public and passengers at all time, the girls must bear this in mind, with a view to being very polite and rendering complete service to passengers. Watch them closely and see that their requirements are taken care of if at all possible. Stewardesses are aboard planes to care for the passengers at all times, and it is up to the girls to keep an eye on the passengers rather than let the passengers always ask for what they want. Stewardesses should offer pillows, blankets, ash trays, drinking water, adjusting chairs, offering magazine, or writing materials. They must be on the alert for air sickness and offer wax containers or escort passengers to lavatory when necessary.

Runs

Stewardesses must remain with planes at all times and under no circumstances are they to use their own judgement about taking off in some other plane when stranded at intermediate points on account of bad weather or otherwise.

The runs of all Stewardesses will be adhered to as at present and no switches in runs are to be made without approval from the Chief Stewardess at Cheyenne.

The runs of all Stewardesses are supervised and regulated from the master control board in office of the General Superintendent at Cheyenne, where all movements are known at all times.

Uniforms

Uniforms consist of two kinds; the field uniform, being the dark green outfit of four pieces, namely cape, coat, skirt and green beret. The onboard uniform consists of light gray cotton smock and gray nurse's cap. These are to be worn aboard at all times in an orderly manner, when weather permits.

Uniforms should be pressed occasionally and cleaned about once a month. Smocks and caps to be laundered after each trip.

In addition there is a leather coat provided for cold weather.

Gray hose and black medium heeled shoes complete the uniform. We must have uniform dress, however, and all colors and apparel must be exactly alike.

Only cleanly starched smocks and caps are to be worn aboard, and these to be changed at once with spare one aboard, if soiled. Change can be made into field uniform just before debarking.

Air Sickness

Nothing spoils a trip more than air sickness and we caution all Stewardesses regarding this. All girls must carry a supply of Amytal and the Ammonia Inhalant at all times. The latter are found very useful in checking nausea, and the former having a quieting effect.

Cabin Cleanliness

Keep the cabin immaculate at all times. Dust easily forms on window sills and girls should dust off, often. A small broom is provided to assist in keeping the floor clean.

Smoking

Cigarette smoking only permitted aboard, and we provide ash trays for this purpose. Be very careful at all times regarding fire.

Liquor aboard Planes

There must be no drinking by passengers aboard planes and, of course, no passengers are to be accepted that appear inebriated or boisterous. If drinking is attempted aboard, stewardess will politely request that passengers desist. In the event of any unpleasantries, which are very unlikely if properly handled, stewardess will call co-pilot.

Information to Passengers

Stewardesses are expected to be as familiar as possible with their run and able to answer any ordinary questions at all times concerning the run, points of interest, times, objects below, mileage, distances, altitudes, etc.

Carry on conversation with passengers when approached, but otherwise it is not desirable to promote this. Some passengers prefer to keep quiet.

Principal objects below should be pointed out to passengers that appear interested or are not sleeping.

Girls should be familiar with our speed, horse power of motor, gasoline consumption, price and weight of planes, etc.

LOST ARTICLES

Lost articles found aboard planes or in waiting rooms will be turned into the Company, preferably the field manager at either Oakland, Cheyenne or Chicago.

BAGGAGE

Nothing is more aggravating than lost baggage, so adhere closely to the standard regulations and forms we have in this regard, such as checking baggage, writing designations clearly, listing the complete lot on our baggage report forms, checking aboard, etc. Great personal care must be paid to this point.

NAMES OF PASSENGERS

Learn all passengers' names as soon as possible from tickets and address them accordingly as this is a little personal touch of appeal.

PASSENGERS

There is only one class of passenger, and all are guests of our Company, and all are to be treated accordingly at all times, even to the smallest child.

Women passengers should receive special care, as we desire to cater to ladies at all times. See that their wants are taken care of.

LAVATORY

Keep this clean at all times and inspect often, and use the deodorant aboard when necessary.

TICKETS

Stewardesses are to handle and collect all passengers' tickets and punch ticket at each point enroute as passed.

MEDICAL STORES

Each stewardess will carry the few designated medical stores in bag at all times, including Amytal, a supply of Ammonia Inhalants, a small bottle of Ergot and a few sanitary napkins.

FIRST AID KIT

Check the first aid kits aboard planes each trip and make sure that they are complete. We have a reserve supply at Cheyenne and anything short can be replaced at once.

DEODORANT

A supply of Odornox is aboard each plane, and is to use freely in lavatory and/or other places at the discretion of Stewardess.

READING MATTER ABOARD

Stewardesses are to keep a few current popular magazines with them in leather bags for use of passengers. Buy these occasionally and put on expense accounts. Keep magazines up to date, getting such as Life, Judge, Cosmopolitan, Red Book, etc. We notice that passengers do not go in for heavy reading but prefer something very light.

CONTROL OF SHIP

The Operating Department operates all equipment and, accordingly, the pilot is in direct command of plane at all times, and anything of an unusual nature must be reported by Stewardess to the pilot at once. Carry out pilot's instructions implicitly at all times.

TELEGRAMS

Be sure to solicit all passengers concerning telegrams 20 minutes or more before each stop. It is the sending of wires by passengers after we arrive at stations that complicates and delays departures, etc. All wires should be written out and paid for in advance by passengers to Stewardess. If each Stewardess has not up-to-date telegraph tariff for this purpose, get one at once from Cheyenne. This point is very important. Solicit all in advance. Keep supply of telegraph blanks on hand in bag. Turn in collected funds to point where message is sent.

RAILROAD SCHEDULES

Each stewardess must acquire immediately one railroad schedule of each railway or connecting railroad or bus line along route. For instance, Oakland–Salt Lake girls must have Southern Pacific, Union Pacific and Western Pacific folders in bag at all times. Chicago girls should have New York Central, Pennsylvania, Milwaukee, as well as Union Pacific schedules in bag at all times, in addition to bus line and other connecting carriers' schedules. Often passengers want this information enroute and it must be available immediately on board. Each Stewardess must check this at once.

CONNECTING AIR LINE SCHEDULES

Often passengers desire to make a connection by some other airline and stewardesses must assist passengers in working out connections by reference to the "Aviation Guide," supplied monthly to each field manager along the line.

FORCED LANDINGS

In the event of forced landings, pilot and/or co-pilot is in complete charge at all times, but the stewardess must assist in every way with the care and aid of passengers. This also applies to assisting passengers with rail or other transportation connections when necessary, looking out for their baggage, etc.

CONDUCT OF STEWARDESSES

Stewardesses are to conduct themselves in a lady-like and dignified manner at all times consistent with Boeing System policy. Be careful about loud laughing or talking, or any boisterous conversations. We want the stewardesses to act like perfect ladies at all times, as this was the purpose of the service—to create a psychological effect with the public.

EXPENSE ACCOUNTS

Render expense accounts weekly for week ending Saturday night to the chief stewardess at Cheyenne for the past seven days. Include meals and hotels while away from home port at the rate of not to exceed $2 per day for meals and $2 for hotel. Expense accounts also include valet service on uniforms, laundry on smocks when necessary, and what few incidentals like magazines that are occasionally necessary; also automobile charges when absolutely necessary, but this last must be kept to an absolute minimum. Girls can usually get back and forth from fields with regular passenger cars or mail cars, as a rule.

MEAL SERVICE

Meal service aboard continues as at present, with hampers and with all through passengers, pay or pass, eating. But this system is to be shortly changed, when hampers are to be eliminated, and later bulletin will shortly come out on this subject.

SMOKING AROUND HANGARS

Be careful that passengers do not smoke while ships are gassing at hangars, or while passengers are walking around hangars near ships. Stewardesses should be on the alert for gas leaks at all times, and it would be well to eliminate smoking in cabin for about 30 minutes after gassing.

GUM

See that you have a sufficient supply of the small gum packets for liberal distribution to passengers at all times.

PILLOWS AND BLANKETS

Stow pillow and blankets aboard in racks on both sides alternating blanket and pillow. Blankets to be with insignia on bottom, showing through mesh of rack. Ample room can be arranged for passengers' coats, parcels, etc. by shifting a little when necessary.

ADJUSTING ALTIMETERS

Altimeters in ships vary with the barometer, and they should be adjusted to show correct altitude before taking off from any main point. Passengers find it very interesting to observe these altimeters and we must keep them accurate. A few altitudes include Oakland, 0; Reno, 4500; Salt Lake City, 4250; Cheyenne, 6100; Omaha, 1200; and Chicago, 650.

WINDING OF CLOCKS

It is the duty of the outgoing stewardess to see that clocks are properly wound and correct time showing, to show Pacific, Mountain or Central time.

HEAD GEAR

No stewardess is to be without some sort of head gear at all times, either beret or gray uniform cap; never bare-headed.

ESCORTING PASSENGERS

Upon pulling into each station along the line, stewardesses follow the procedure of assisting the passengers out and then escorting them into the waiting rooms; never into any other door but the entrance to the waiting rooms. Passengers, under no circumstances, are allowed in any of our offices or radio rooms of any of the stations.

Relief for Chief Stewardess at Cheyenne

When found necessary for chief stewardess to take any runs, substituting for other girls, then whatever Chicago girls are in Cheyenne will be on duty at the airport office representing the chief stewardess in the usual matters of routine, traffic, etc. The Chicago girl that gets in Cheyenne at night will go to the airport office the next morning and hold that down until both tri-motors have cleared through that same evening. This girl must follow arrival of planes, meal services required, check linen and handle all traffic matters such as tickets, baggage, etc. and handle the passengers.

Safety Belts

Stewardesses are to see that passengers adjust and use safety belts whenever indications are that weather will be rough. If any safety belts are out of order or missing, be sure to report on daily report.

Portfolios

Portfolios should be kept supplied with airgrams, blotters, air mail stamps, etc. at all times, and offered to the passengers enroute. These portfolios should be available at all times, as we welcome passengers' writing airgrams from the air while enroute. Stewardesses must render every service in collecting and mailing airgrams and supplying postage stamps.

Linen

Articles such as napkins, towels, etc. will be issued clean at the commencement of each trip, similar to as at present, with supplies at Oakland, Cheyenne and Chicago, and a supplementary supply at Salt Lake.

Stewardesses' Addresses

Addresses and phone numbers must always be left with field managers at home ports, intermediate stops and Cheyenne for emergency calls at all times.

BEFORE DEPARTURE

Stewardess will report at field for duty at least 45 minutes before plane departure. Make a thorough inspection of cabin; advise field manager of anything lacking or out or order. Place back covers on seats and place blankets and pillows on board. Secure list of passengers from field manager. See that all baggage is properly tagged and placed aboard plane. Fill out baggage form report in duplicate. Escort passengers to plane. Collect main body of ticket or pass from passengers. Inspect hamper to see that everything is accounted for. Permit no baggage or loose articles to remain on the floor in rear of cabin; if insufficient room in baggage compartment, have baggage placed in forward part of cabin.

ENROUTE

When taking off, see that everyone remains seated; same for landing. Immediately after take-off change to smock uniform. Inspect cabin to see that parcels, wraps, etc. are removed from seats and placed in racks. See that each passenger is comfortable; give each passenger a gum packet. Lock entrance door of cabin after take-off. Unlock door before turning down to land. Watch passengers going to lavatory to see that they do not open outside door.

ARRIVAL

About 15 minutes before arrival, notify passengers accordingly. Remain in your seat and instruct passenger to do likewise until plane is landed. Escort passengers to dining-room, waiting-room, etc. Examine cabin for personal effects left by passengers. Escort passengers to departing planes. Advise passengers approximate length of stop. Upon arrival at any intermediate point, and Cheyenne, stewardess will give field manager list of "off" passengers at that stop.

HANDLING PASSENGERS (CHEYENNE)

Advise passengers 15 or 20 minutes before time of landing: approximate time of stop; restaurant service; that they will be called from restaurant in time to make plane; receive any telegrams to be sent before landing.

Upon arrival in Cheyenne: escort passengers to restaurant; indicate rest rooms. Inspect cabin for parcels left; ascertain from field manager length of stop; advise passengers time for dining; advise passengers five minutes before departure; escort passengers to outbound plane.

REPORTS

There were numerous reports that the stewardess was required to file at the end of her run, including reports for baggage, lost articles, cabin conditions, unusual occurrences, passengers, medical, expenses, and equipment.[32]

STEWARDESS MANUAL REVISIONS 1933

On January 1, 1933, Boeing Air Transport officials issued a revised stewardess manual with a few changes noted as follows, with an introductory statement:

The Boeing Division, from the inception of its passenger service, has striven to maintain the highest possible standard of service to its passengers. It is, of course, obviously impossible to incorporate in this brief booklet, the exact duties of each stewardess. The season of the year, the time of day, the weather, the passengers, and many other conditions enter into the circumstances which govern this service, and make it most necessary for the stewardess to use her own common sense and good judgment when necessary. Air transportation is still new and precedence is lacking in many cases, we must rely upon the initiative and ability of our various employees.

We, by all means, invite and welcome suggestions and criticisms from our stewardesses, as it is they who are in intimate contact with the passengers during flight, and from these suggestions we expect to still further improve the service wherever possible.[33]

The runs for the transcontinental route of Boeing Aircraft were divided into four routes. They were San Francisco/Oakland to Salt Lake City, Salt Lake City to Cheyenne, Cheyenne to Omaha and Omaha to Chicago.

Steve Stimpson (*center*), writer of the first stewardess manual; stewardess Jean Clarke (*left*) in a 1950 winter uniform; and stewardess Charlotte Schade in a 1933 uniform are shown reading an updated stewardess manual. *United Air Lines.*

A few of the changes in some categories of the 1933 stewardess manual are as follows:

UNIFORMS

The stewardess uniform consists of a dark green outfit of four pieces, namely, coat, skirt, cape and beret. White blouses are worn in the summertime, and white or light colored shirts with green tie in the wintertime. Dark hose and medium heeled, black oxfords are to be worn with the uniform at all times. The complete uniform is to be worn at all times when the stewardess is on duty.

DUTIES

Duties remain the same with this addition: The stewardess will see that passengers adjust and use seat belts whenever indications are that weather will be rough, and at take-offs and landings. Report any seat belts out of order or missing. Refer to belts as "SEAT BELTS" only, not Safety Belts.

SMOKING

Cigarette smoking only is permitted aboard planes.

There will be absolutely no smoking permitted during landings and take-offs, or in planes which are being serviced or idle at stations. Neither will smoking be permitted in hangars or loading sheds.

"No Smoking" signs should be hung on the forward wall of the cabin prior to take-off and remain in that position until several minutes after take-off and/or until any and all gas fumes have distinctly disappeared. Similarly, a few minutes before any landing is made the sign will be properly hung up and will remain in that position the entire time the plane is on the ground.

Passengers who may be violating the instructions should be courteously requested to abide by the sign.

When the sign is removed, it will not be merely reversed, but will be put away, either on the rack or in your equipment case, where easy access to it may be had.

MEDICAL

In addition to making sure first aid kits are aboard the aircraft each stewardess is to carry these supplies in her equipment case: 25 Aspirin; 12 Amytal; 1 tube of Alkaline Effervescent; and 12 Aromatic Ammonia ampules.

Stewardesses are advised to waken any sleeping passengers when coming in for a landing due to the possibility that ear drums may rupture if the pressure is not equalized by swallowing or yawning when losing altitude.

LINENS AND PASSENGER EQUIPMENT

Each trimotor plane should include passenger equipment as follows: 6 or 7 magazines in binders; 6 towels; 15 pillows; 15 pillow slips; 15 pillow protection covers; and 15 seat back covers.

The food supply is to include: 1 tin hamper box; 6 food trays; 1 large (1 gallon) Thermos bottle; 2 (2 quart) Thermos bottles; 1 (½ pint) Thermos bottle; 15 cups wrapped in wax paper; 6 cup holders; and 1 fruit basket.

GUM

A sufficient supply of gum packets will be carried for distribution to passengers. A reserve supply is kept at Cheyenne.

MAGAZINES

At departure from Cheyenne, Oakland and Chicago, stewardess will place on board six or seven magazines provided, enclosed in binders. These magazines will go to the end of the run where they will be turned in to the field office for future use. Those binders and magazines should not be permitted to lay over at stations for any length of time for it is necessary that the binders be carried into Cheyenne regularly in order that new issues may be placed in them as published.

STATIONERY SUPPLIES

Supplies of post cards, stationery, and blotters will be kept on hand at all times, and offered to passengers enroute. Stewardesses should render service in mailing letters, post cards, etc.

CAB TRANSPORTATION

Stewardess should ascertain from each passenger, whether or not he will desire cab transportation at his destination. If cab is desired, stewardess will so inform the field manager at the preceding station in order that he may in turn advise the passenger's destination terminal in ample time to cause no delay to the passenger upon arrival, and also to eliminate the necessity of using the plane's radio service for this purpose. The passenger should understand, of course, that cab transportation in such instances is at his own expense.

SAFETY FIRST CARDS

As you know, quite often when planes are delayed on account of weather, some of the passengers being transported strenuously object to the delay, and frequently insinuate that the pilot is lying down on the job and could go on if he desired. Delays of this kind are, of course, in the interest of safety, and in order to better impress this fact on the minds of the passengers, our Publicity Department has had a supply of "Safety First" cards printed which are to be carried by our stewardess personnel and given out to passengers when a weather delay occurs, if circumstances warrant.

You will therefore see that an adequate supply of these cards is carried in your equipment case at all times for distribution as stated. Stock will be kept on hand at Oakland, Salt Lake and Cheyenne.

REPORTS

Stewardess's reports include a Cabin Report, Report of Unusual Occurrences, Detail Report, Passenger Report, Passenger Manifest, and Medical Reports. Perhaps the most interesting of these was the Report of Unusual Occurrences that stated: Report will be made in detail of any exceptional occurrence happening enroute or at stations concerning passengers. Such as injury, peculiar conduct, annoyance by one passenger to another, extraordinary or severe illness, etc., or any other occurrence which should be called to the attention of the office. This report should be forwarded immediately to Operations Headquarters by the stewardess.

EXPENSE ACCOUNTS

Render account weekly for the week ending Saturday night, for the past seven days, to the Operations Headquarters at Cheyenne. Expense accounts are to include meals while away from home port at the rate of not to exceed $2.00 per day. Meals put in for portion of day are not to exceed the following prices: Breakfast, 50 cents; Lunch 75 cents; Dinner 75 cents. Expense for lodging will be claimed on the first expense account of each month to cover lodging expense for the current month, where apartments have been rented. Include also expenditures for cab transportation of passengers and

A group of unidentified stewardesses poses on the wing of an airplane, circa 1930s. *United Air Lines.*

meals in connection therewith on forced landings or delays. Receipts for meals and lodging at other than regular stops will be submitted with expense accounts. Cab transportation at foreign stations will be allowed only when company transportation is not available, and on such occasions approval of the field manager will be obtained. Miscellaneous expense incurred will be fully explained on the back of the Expense Account sheet.[34]

In addition to the many items included in the stewardess training manual, the airline industry in general was changing rapidly.

The duties and responsibilities of the stewardess continued to gain importance within all United States airlines. In the 1930s, aircraft changed radically; therefore, the stewardesses needed to receive updated information. With each new plane type, new considerations for passenger comfort had to be addressed. While greater comfort and efficiency went a long way in helping the stewardesses make the flights a pleasant experience, the increased capacity each plane carried and the variety of new ways airlines competed with one another in terms of customer service placed even greater demands on the women.

In July 1934, Boeing Air Transport combined with Pacific Air Transport, National Air Transport and Varney Airlines to form United Air Lines.

When stewardess service was initiated in 1930, the planes were slow and noisy, offering a less than ideal passenger experience. The Boeing trimotor Model 80 carried twelve passengers in a boxy interior with wicker seats, though it did attempt to provide a pleasing interior with wood paneling and amenities designed to replicate a train coach.

By 1933, Boeing had developed a comfortable and quiet plane in the Boeing 247 aircraft. The cabin featured five seats with fixed armrests spaced a generous forty inches apart on each side of a single aisle. There was a galley and restroom in the rear of the plane. The streamlined all-metal 247 could fly coast to coast in less than a day. United Air Lines agreed to purchase sixty of the new planes. However, when other airlines attempted to order the new planes, they were told they would have to

An unidentified stewardess serves food aboard the Boeing 247 plane. *United Air Lines.*

wait until all the United planes had been delivered. These other airlines then turned to Douglas Aircraft Company for planes. Unfortunately for Boeing, the Douglas DC-1, DC-2 and DC-3 planes proved to be superior to the Boeing 247. The 247 was eventually phased out at United Air Lines in favor of the Douglas aircraft by 1935. Boeing, of course, went on to develop more significant aircraft in later years.[35]

Meanwhile, stewardesses were learning the skills needed to attend to passengers on the new DC airlines being put into service. In 1936, United placed the DC-3 twin-engine airplane into service. This innovative twenty-one-seat aircraft was sometimes called the first modern airliner. It could span the United States with four or five fuel stops. Stewardesses served hot meals on board. The equipment was more efficient, and the flying time coast to coast dropped to twenty-two hours, down from the Boeing 247's twenty-seven hours of flight time.[36]

Some of the twenty-one-seat DC-3s were converted to fourteen-passenger deluxe liners featuring large upholstered wing chairs. Others were converted into sleeper planes containing seven compartments. Six

A group of stewardesses poses in front of the Douglas DC-3 aircraft in 1939. *United Air Lines.*

Passengers on United Air Lines overnight DC-3 sleeper planes traveled in style. Stewardesses served breakfast in bed, and then passengers changed clothing in a luxurious lounge while their berths were made. Upper berths folded into the ceiling; lower berths converted into two facing seats. By day, stewardesses served meals on crisp white linen and fine china, with bouquets of fresh flowers at each table. *United Air Lines.*

compartments could be transformed into berths, an upper and a lower in each group. The seventh compartment was a lounge. Food service aboard these aircraft was elaborate, with several courses served on tables with china, sterling silver and fine linens. The company had discovered that food had become important in competing with other airlines for passengers. United spent $5,000 in 1936 to open the industry's first flight kitchen in Oakland, California. Within a few days, the first hot meals were served aboard a DC-3. The meals were kept hot in an electrically heated compartment designed by United's engineers. The meals were wrapped in heavy paper to provide insulation and packed in a paper box that doubled as a lap tray.[37]

With the success of the DC-3, the stewardess position became a permanent airline occupation. United Air Lines opened a formal stewardess training center in Chicago in 1936. Qualifications for stewardesses were also updated. As planes became larger and more technologically advanced, these new requirements were put into practice:

> A United Air Lines Stewardess must be a citizen of the United States and single or a widow with no children. She must be at least five feet two inches and not over five feet seven inches in height, and weigh 135 pounds, or less, proportionately. She must have attained her 21st birthday and not yet reached her 27th birthday. Each applicant is required to pass a rigid physical examination approved by the Medical Department of United Air Lines to make certain that she has not physical abnormalities that would impair or tend to impair her usefulness for flying duty. One of the more important physical requirements is satisfactory vision without glasses. The wearing of glasses while in uniform is not permitted. Applications are now accepted from girls who are either registered nurses or who have completed at least two years of college, or one year of college, plus one year of business experience.[38]

United Air Lines continued to evolve, and new technology was incorporated frequently. Larger airplanes were acquired, and with the introduction of Douglas aircraft there were many changes.

As the age of passenger service grew, the advent of World War II intervened to cause additional modifications that affected United Air Lines.

MODIFICATION CENTER, CHEYENNE, WYOMING

Aviation activities at Cheyenne expanded rapidly. Most important was the United Air Lines Modification Center, which installed new guns and instruments and otherwise modified thousands of B-17 Flying Fortresses and smaller numbers of other bombers. Two huge hangars were built for the work in 1942, and additional improvements were made in 1943. The modification center employed 1,600 people, half of them women, working in three different shifts around the clock.[39]

In the spring of 1942, United turned over half of its fleet of airplanes and ground equipment to the government. The planes were used to transport soldiers and deliver vital equipment around the world. There was a desperate need for bombers in all combat theaters at the beginning of the war.

To fulfill the need for bombers, United transformed its massive maintenance facility in Cheyenne, Wyoming, into a bomber modification center. The workers at Modification Center Number 10 made last-minute alterations such as installing machine gun mounts, rebuilding tail turret assemblies and installing additional equipment. Two sixty-four-thousand-square-foot hangars were built to shelter the scores of bombers being worked on. By the conclusion of the war, the Cheyenne operation had manufactured over 4 million aircraft parts and had prepared 5,736 B-17s for combat.[40]

Thousands of B-17 airplanes were altered at the Cheyenne Modification Center for combat assignments in many theaters during World War II. During the first six months of 1943, an average of six planes left Cheyenne for operational duty every day.[41]

Once the plant opened in Cheyenne, thousands of people came to the city to work at the facility, causing a housing shortage. Every extra room and basement in the city were occupied by the workers. Some were forced to find housing in other nearby towns. Eventually, temporary housing for the workers was built in several locations around Cheyenne. However, once the war ended, most of the workers left Cheyenne.

The importance of the Cheyenne municipal airport declined significantly following the end of the war and the closing of the modification center. Technology and the demand for efficiency in transportation led to the demise of an airport that had been one of the finest in the nation and one of the principal centers of the airline industry.[42]

However, Cheyenne was not finished with the glory days of aviation. Training for varied groups of personnel was scheduled to operate in Cheyenne, including passenger agents, reservation agents, sales agents and managers. Soon, hundreds of young women would spend several weeks of their lives living in Cheyenne as they entered a bright new career for women that turned into a legacy for the airline industry.

3

Cheyenne's Friendly Skies

Following the end of World War II, Cheyenne's modification center shifted into a peacetime role for United Air Lines. Hundreds of jobs related to the airline industry in Cheyenne were lost when the modification center was no longer in operation, and other facilities were also moved to different locations.

United Air Lines had expanded its routes in 1947 by inaugurating flights to Hawaii, made possible by the large and powerful DC-6 aircraft. The DC-4 was a new civilian airliner modeled after the powerful wartime C-54 Skymaster. A large aircraft with four engines, the plane boasted a pressurized cabin, modern avionics and the ability to fly over four thousand miles in a single flight. Importantly, the new plane could carry fifty-seven passengers. After the introduction of the DC-6, Cheyenne's maintenance facility was moved to San Francisco to a new center that was specifically tailored for the advanced aircraft. United also moved its flight training program to Denver.

The loss of the United Air Lines facilities in Cheyenne caused difficulties for the citizens of the town. Hundreds of jobs had been lost, and there seemed very little hope that they would return. There was, however, a silver lining to the community's predicament. The new plane, with its vast new potential, opened the floodgates for modern aviation. The demand for crew trained to take care of the thousands of new passengers grew exponentially, and Cheyenne was about to receive a very welcome reprieve.

A stewardess hands out newspapers to passengers on board a Boeing 247 plane on November 22, 1937. *Wyoming State Archives, Department of State Parks and Cultural Resources.*

Following the closure of much of its Cheyenne operations, United Air Lines recognized the value of the long-term relationship it had maintained with the City of Cheyenne and decided not to abandon it completely, offering to relocate its stewardess school to Cheyenne. The move coincided with the expansion of United's facilities in Chicago. The stewardess training center in Chicago, established in 1936, had been demolished to provide space for more hangars, thus making it necessary to find new quarters for the school.

There was an urgency in United Air Lines' desire to reopen a stewardess school. With the ending of the war, a huge new demand for air travel was born. Thousands of veterans returning from the war had experienced air travel during their service. Instead of being a rather daring venture, travel by air for business or leisure made perfect sense to this new generation of travelers. Airlines scrambled to meet the demand. For United's part, its managers calculated that the airline would need six hundred new stewardesses annually. This was not only to meet the demand but also to compensate for the attrition of stewardess ranks due to marriage.[43]

The news of the relocation of the stewardess school to Cheyenne was of much interest to the city. The *Wyoming State Tribune* published the following article:

> Plans for United Air Lines is to consolidate its entire ground training program at Cheyenne, with an average monthly total of 500 students and staff members to be here by July, 1947, were announced today by W.P. Hoare, manager of the company's Cheyenne maintenance base.
>
> Mr. Hoare said that United will build dormitories, classrooms and office facilities for educational training work in the company's former modification center here. Also, approximately $75,000 worth of training equipment will be brought here.
>
> As one of the first moves, United will transfer 50 families to Cheyenne from Chicago and other points where ground training has been conducted in the past. The training is expected to get underway here this summer.
>
> Included in the program will be preparatory, supplementary and apprentice training of the kind with which United indoctrinates new employes [sic] and keeps them up-to-date with new advancements in their jobs and in the airline industry as a whole. On-the-job training will continue to be given at points along the line as in the past.
>
> Preparatory training includes indoctrination, wire operator instruction and passenger-traffic instruction. The supplementary training consists of short-term, concentrated courses for up-grading other than new employes. Apprentice training is a four-year program for the development of mechanical personnel.
>
> United's education service department is under the overall supervision of R.F. Ahrens, vice president in charge of personnel. D.B. Wodyatt is superintendent of educational service with T. Lee, Jr., in charge of training programs.
>
> Personnel who will be coming to Cheyenne for training will include passenger agents, reservation agents, stewardesses, counter sales agents, wire operators and mechanics. Mr. Hoare said that an immediate problem will be that of obtaining adequate housing facilities for staff members.[44]

United Air Lines placed Jack Hayes in charge of the transfer of the stewardess school from Chicago to Cheyenne. Hayes had joined United in 1937 and performed various jobs for the company in several different cities. He eventually became instructor at the airline's training school in Chicago and was involved with the training of pilots, stewardesses and ground crews.

Hayes was not enthusiastic about being transferred to Cheyenne, a place he considered to "be a small town in the middle of nowhere." Hayes arrived in Cheyenne in 1947 to find the facility to be used for the stewardess school was in disarray, with a great deal of residue left over from the war-era modification center operations that previously occupied the location. Hayes said cleaning the building and getting it ready for the stewardess candidates was a big job. The upper level of the three-story brick building was converted into dormitories and training rooms for the students. Hayes was delighted to find out the cafeteria, located in a separate building, was still in existence.[45]

In addition to stewardess training in Cheyenne, United established an education and training center designed to broaden the talents of both management and non-management personnel. Personal development and management instruction included lectures and conferences examining the topics of leadership, human behavior, self-analysis and improvement and communications. A decade after Jack Hayes arrived in Cheyenne, he served as superintendent of management training. Other leaders by 1957 included R.E. Parish, supervisor of field training, and Tom Pierson, supervisor of stewardess training.[46]

Even though Jack Hayes had not been excited about his move to Cheyenne, over the years, he seems to have become enamored with both the friendly skies and friendly people of Wyoming. In many issues of the *United Air Lines News*, he is noted as having enjoyed fishing and hunting, and once was referred to as "Cactus" Jack Hayes, who was making hunting plans, in a November 1948 news column.[47]

The February 1950 edition of the UAL contained this report:

> *Senior instructor Jack Hayes first job with UAL, back in 1937, was washing Boeing aircraft. Since then he has worked as Station Agent, Radio Operator, Dispatch Clerk, Assistant Station Manager, Station Manager, Ramp Control Chief, Instructor, and Senior Instructor at nine UAL stations. Thus he's an authority on almost anything pertaining to ground operations. Jack is an enthusiastic hunter, fisherman and rancher on his El Rancho eight-acre place two miles out of town. But, his first love is amateur radio. During last winter's blizzard, he took an active part in Operation Snowbound, as the local emergency corps handled private message traffic for marooned travelers.*[48]

Hayes was also often mentioned in news about social events in and around Cheyenne, including acting as the director of the annual Christmas party at the Little Bear Inn. The Inn was one of the favorite places for stewardesses to spend time during their leisure hours.

In the course of his tenure in Cheyenne, Hayes grew to love the area. He and his wife raised two children on the south side of the city and on weekends drove them through the nearby mountains. When the Cheyenne Stewardess School closed in 1961, Hayes continued working for United Air Lines in Denver. He returned to Cheyenne in 1973 when he retired, saying, "My family and I appreciated the Wyoming lifestyle."[49]

By the late summer of 1947, the Cheyenne airfield was busy with many activities, including management training and the establishment of the Cheyenne Stewardess School. Managers stated that young women intent on earning the silver wings of a stewardess would learn in-flight procedures, company history and policy, regulations, first aid, geography, airline routes and codes, charm and grooming.

The first stewardesses hired in 1930 were required to be registered graduate nurses. This requirement remained in force until World War II, when, with nurses needed for duties in the military, the airlines waived their nurse requirement. In its place, they substituted college and business training.

Other qualifications for new stewardesses had changed slightly. When the training center opened in Cheyenne, requirements included either a registered nurse certificate or two years of college, or one year of college and one year of business experience. Each candidate was required to be a citizen of the United States, unmarried, between five feet, two inches and five feet, seven inches in height, 135 pounds or less in weight and between twenty-one and twenty-six years of age.

Every new stewardess was required to undergo an intensive training course at the company's special training school in Cheyenne. They were furnished transportation to the Cheyenne training school, where their education was provided without cost, including daily meals in the company cafeteria and lodging in the training center dormitories. They also received one dollar per day in subsistence pay.

Classroom instruction included lectures, often from veteran stewardesses reassigned for the task, use of visual training aids and actual practice of in-flight duties. Students learned to fill out report forms as though they had completed actual flights. Instruction in food service included simulated practice of the meals served from a full-scale working model like the food buffet on planes. They learned how individual food trays are set up on the ground and the quickest way to prepare the meals for service aloft. Students also practiced the proper method of serving meals.

An outside view of the United Air Lines Stewardess Training Center in Cheyenne, Wyoming, circa 1950s. Notice the station wagon in the front used to take stewardesses on outings in the Cheyenne area. *Courtesy of Patricia Seibel Romeo.*

A training class at the United Air Lines school in Cheyenne, Wyoming. *United Air Lines.*

Additional studies included company history, principles of flight, mechanism of the plane, weather, traffic and ticketing procedures. Candidates received a firsthand view of the flight deck of a United Mainliner and learned about the engines, instrument panels and more.[50]

The *Stewardess Manual* published on February 1, 1947, contained many updates, including the following items:

INTRODUCTION

The degree of success to be attained by a stewardess in performing the type of service expected of her depends largely upon the interest which she takes in her work. Over a period of time, even on one flight, a stewardess meets a great variety of personalities. One passenger may be taking advantage of the speed provided by our service to reach the sick bed of a relative or friend; another passenger may be on a vacation flight; and still another may be a business man to whom flying is an everyday experience. In dealing with passengers, the stewardess must recognize and understand difference in temperament and circumstances, and govern her actions accordingly.

United Air Lines has attained a position of leadership in the field of air transportation because of its progressiveness and its interest in providing the highest standards of service. Particular emphasis is placed on safety, passenger comfort, speed, and convenience, combined with alert, courteous, and intelligent attention on the part of every employee.

A stewardess with the proper concept of the word "service" and a clear understanding of her duties is in a position to assist greatly in the development of regular "repeat" patronage, which is one of the major factors in the success of any transportation system.

REQUIREMENTS FOR EMPLOYMENT

It is necessary that the stewardess be tactful, gracious, resourceful, and patient in her relations with the public and with other employees. She should have poise, a neat and attractive appearance, and a pleasant manner, and will be required to meet high mental, moral, and physical standards.

Each applicant must either be a registered nurse or must have completed at least two years of college or university work. Training

Stewardesses posed on a baggage cart driven by a classmate during training at the Cheyenne school, circa 1950s. *Wyoming State Archives, Department of State Parks and Cultural Resources.*

in physiology or hygiene, psychology, sociology, home economics, foreign languages, or music or art is highly desirable....

One of the more important physical requirements is satisfactory vision, since the wearing of glasses while on duty is not permitted. Each stewardess must be a citizen of the United States, and must be unmarried.

PASSENGER ACCOMMODATIONS

The Mainliner 180 [UAL's designation for the DC-3 and the dominant plane of the era] is a 21 passenger airplane. The seats are arranged in three rows of seven seats each, with a single row on the right-hand side and a double row on the left-hand side of the cabin. Ash trays are located on the wall by all window seats, on the center armrest of all double seats, and in the lavatory. Stewardess call buttons, reading lights and switches, and individual fresh air inlets are located on wall panels above windows.

The lavatory is located at the rear of the main entrance door on the right hand side of the cabin. It contains a wash basin and a chemical toilet.

There are racks running the full length of the cabin for hats, coats, and hand luggage on both sides of the fuselage near the ceiling.

The Mainliner 230 is a 48 passenger plane. The seats are arranged in double rows on each side of the aisle. There are two lavatories at the rear of the cabin.

RESPONSIBILITIES

Each stewardess is directly responsible to her chief stewardess for conduct and performance of duties. The comfort and care of passengers aboard the plane will be the primary duty of the stewardess. She will be responsible for maintaining company standards and furthering company progress, and will discharge her duties efficiently and tactfully.

Tips are not to be accepted, and will be declined tactfully and graciously.

Smoking is absolutely prohibited aboard the plane or while in uniform in the public view. The exception is stewardesses may smoke when sitting at a table in a restaurant.

Stewardesses will not indulge in alcoholic beverages (including beer) within the 12 hour period immediately preceding flight departure, nor will they appear in public liquor dispensing places (cocktail bars, etc.) while in uniform. Stewardesses on reserve duty will refrain from alcoholic beverages during such duty.

Stewardesses will not chew gum while on duty.

Conversations with other UAL personnel on duty will be formal and businesslike. Stewardesses will refrain from calling UAL employees by their first names. Such persons will be addressed as "Mr.", "Captain", "Miss", etc.

Stewardesses are not permitted to work in that capacity after marriage.

For many years, stewardesses gave up their careers when they married. In 1936, these stewardesses sat on a baggage carrier near a Douglas DC-3 plane and pledged, "I will not leap in Leap Year." *United Air Lines.*

GENERAL HINTS

Be alert at all times. Sleeping, smoking, reading, or writing personal letters while on duty is sufficient cause for immediate disciplinary action and possible dismissal from company service, regardless of the number of passengers on board at the time.

Be cheerful and agreeable while on duty. Do not become excited under any conditions. If you appear calm during an irregularity, it will do much to allay uneasiness among passengers.

Acquaint yourself in a general way with the speed, horsepower of engines, radio, airway facilities, etc., in order that you may discuss such information in an intelligent manner. Don't try to be technical, it is not expected of you.

Learn the route over which you fly, including principal towns, river, mountains, scenic points of interest, etc.

Do not enter the station office except on business. Loitering around passenger agent's office, ticket counters, waiting rooms, etc., is prohibited

Use only natural or medium shades of nail polish.

Cologne may be used, but must be of a light and refreshing scent. Perfume is too heavy in the cabin.

Do not wear extreme make-up.

Hair and nails are to be neat. Hair will be styled so as to be above the collar.

Use toilet preparations and mouth wash to maintain daintiness and pleasant breath.

MAINLINER SUPPLIES

Service and First Aid Kits include standard supplies.

Each baby kit is equipped to serve three babies. All items are to be clean. Each baby kit contained milk, fruit, cereal, vegetables, soup and graham crackers. Equipment included 3 spoons, 1 can opener, 1 bottle of baby oil, 1 can of baby powder, 6 diaper bags, 6 diapers, 1 lap pad, 2 baby bibs, and 3 bowls.

There was also a "Baby's Log Book in Flight," a souvenir to be filled in by the crew, certifying that the baby was aboard a Mainliner on a certain date.

Oxygen Kits Contain masks and mouthpieces.

Each writing portfolio will contain 1 clean blue blotter; 1 package air mail stickers;1 sharpened pencil; 10 Western Union telegraph blanks; 25 sheets stationery; 12 plain envelopes; 12 air mail envelopes; and 6 assorted post cards.[51]

While many of these considerations were evidence of United's concern for passengers' comfort and flying pleasure, the new stewardesses found greater emphasis than ever on the proper serving of food.

DINING SERVICE, GENERAL DIRECTIONS

The passenger's pleasure is the basis for all decisions as to the method of serving food in the air. Tempting, well-prepared food, a carefully arranged table, and unobtrusive, efficient service all contribute to the

A stewardess preparing food in the galley of an airplane. *United Air Lines.*

passenger's enjoyment. His wants always should be anticipated and everything possible should be done to make him feel comfortable.

It is preferable to serve food on the planes as near as possible to the way it would be served in any of the better hotels or restaurants. There will, of course, be a few deviations from set rules for serving because of limited time and space. Whenever advisable, food should be served without paper wrapping or covers, but it never should appear as if it has been handled. Anything that can be done in arranging food supplies or equipment so that the work is convenient will improve the service. Evidences of haste or of trying to work in a cluttered buffet detract from the effectiveness of the meal and tend to make passengers uncomfortable.

In order to avoid mishaps and possible company liability, stewardesses will serve all food and drinks without passengers' assistance.

As a general rule, the time of day should be considered in serving meals. If a flight leaves near the meal hour, duties should be arranged so that passengers can be served as soon as possible after departure. This is especially true on flights where a hot meal is served. In order to avoid any difficulty in service due to rough air, the captain should be consulted before serving.

If it appears that the air will be rough during the time when food normally would be served, it is best to ask the passengers if they would like that part of the meal which is convenient to serve under existing conditions. In serving on any plane, begin with the passengers in the rear seats and proceed to the front. A pleasant approach, such as "May I serve you now?" will add much to the passenger's appreciation and enjoyment of the meal. Attention to small details, such as offering the second cup of coffee, removing used dishes quickly, etc., often make a lasting favorable impression. If it is impossible to feed passengers because of rough air, the stewardess will request the captain to advise the next station by radio, so that adequate food service may be provided by that station.

Every effort will be made to include sufficient supplies and food to permit correct United Air Lines service. When irregularities of packing occur, or some food is omitted or does not keep well, dining service must rely upon the stewardess' judgment and tact in making the necessary adjustments. It is preferable to omit a part of the meal rather than to serve food of questionable quality and appearance.

All irregularities should be recorded immediately on "Stewardess Flight Reports" to avoid repetition of factors that lower UAL food standards. Comments of stewardesses and passengers determine, in a large measure, company food policies, and for that reason stewardess' suggestions are quite essential.

Meals served to flight officers will be the same as those served to passengers.

Food will be served to crew members only on trips operating on schedules which make it difficult or impractical for them to eat required meals on the ground. Pilot meal schedules are issued periodically by dining service to indicate flights on which pilot meals will be furnished. If a flight is operating off schedule, the dispatcher is authorized to request necessary meal service for the crew.

Crew members will normally be served only after the stewardess has served all passengers who desire to eat. Upon request of the captain, crew members may be served before passengers when departure is near meal time and crew member have not eaten prior to departure, or when weather makes it advisable for the crew to eat early.

Only one flight officer will eat at a time.

No food will be served to flight officers during rough air conditions or during instrument flight conditions.

Upon request from the cockpit, stewardesses may serve coffee or other liquids to the flight crew between regular passenger meal periods. Such requests are expected to be infrequent. Flight officers will not request meals, coffee, or other liquids during the first half-hour following take-off; during the period when passengers are being served, (unless it is apparent that a scheduled landing will be made prior to completion of passenger serving); or during the half-hour preceding landing.

No metal, wood, or plastic trays, plates, or salt and pepper shakers will be served with food or drink delivered to the cockpit. Wooden or plastic knives, forks, and spoons will be used in place of silverware, and liquids will be served in plastic cups. All food serving equipment with the exception of casseroles will be cardboard. Food serving equipment will be removed from the cockpit as soon as it has served its purpose.[52]

One might assume that, due to the large amount of explanation given to the role of the stewardess in the preparing and distributing of meals, it was always so. As with so many aspects of early travel, the experience was far more colorful. Boeing Air Transport began serving food on flights in 1927. The meal usually consisted of a ham and cheese sandwich and an apple. The co-pilot often handed the food to the passengers as they boarded. Pre-brewed coffee was kept warm in jugs heated by the plane's electrical system. When the Boeing 80 plane came into service in 1929, the standard fare was fried chicken, a bag of potato chips, an apple and a beverage served from a Thermos bottle.

Steve Stimpson quipped, "There never was a co-pilot living who didn't stick his thumb in the coffee, and none of them had a sweet thumb."[53]

When the first stewardesses were hired in 1930, Steve Stimpson, San Francisco traffic manager, said that they had a tremendous effect on the traveling public. He added that the value stewardesses brought to the airline industry included the neater and nicer method of serving food.[54]

Among stewardesses' many tasks, serving meals was one of the most important. Since Prohibition was the law of the land, alcoholic beverages were not served. Stewardesses were asked to warn passengers about sipping from flasks or cough syrup bottles. Even after the end of Prohibition, United Air Lines did not serve alcoholic beverages until 1956. The company president, W.E. Patterson, contended he did not want to turn stewardesses into "flying barmaids." When competition forced the airline to begin serving alcoholic beverages, Patterson stipulated that United would not sell drinks but serve them as hospitality, setting a two-drink limit. Later, the company joined other airlines in charging for alcoholic beverages.[55]

United Air Lines opened the industry's first flight kitchen in Oakland, California, in 1936. The first hot meals were served aboard a DC-3 airline

The Thanksgiving menu served aboard a United Air Lines flight in 1937. *United Air Lines.*

and offered a choice of fried chicken or scrambled eggs. The meals were kept hot in an electrically heated compartment. Each had been wrapped in heavy paper and then packed in a box that doubled as a lap tray. By the 1950s, planes were outfitted with the individual seat tray. Menus and meal service continued to be updated throughout the ensuing years. There were often special menus served especially on the occasion of a holiday.[56]

In 1969, after the introduction of the Boeing-747 jumbo jet, food service was greatly augmented. The food was prepared by the galley staff in the belly of the aircraft. Partially prepared and frozen meals were set up, cooked and arranged on food service carts, which were then taken by elevator to the passenger serving level.[57]

Eventually, sixteen flight kitchens turned out eighty million meals annually. In 1990,

United Air Lines ranked among the largest twenty-five restaurant chains in the nation. However, in 1993, United sold most of its flight kitchens to a catering company.[58]

ILL PASSENGERS

One of the most demanding and unpleasant duties that the new stewardesses had to contend with was the unfortunate and all too frequent necessity of handling passengers who did not take to flying well. The 1947 stewardess manual offered some of the following advice:

AIR SICKNESS

> Air sickness causes may include fear, motion, fatigue, nervousness, worry, odors, rough air or overheated cabins.
> The stewardess may offer comfort by opening air vents; by placing a passenger in a reclining position and offering a pillow and a blanket; give the passenger Seconal for relaxation; use an ammonia inhalant; offer Kleenex; and help the passenger, if necessary, to use the "burp cup" fastened either under the seat or on the seat back.

The one-quart cardboard burp cups at each seat were a necessity. On the DC-3, they were held by a clip underneath each seat. One unfortunate stewardess found out it was unwise to lean over to obtain the burp cup in front of an ill passenger. Just as the unfortunate attendant bent over to retrieve the cup, the passenger vomited all over her. After washing her hair and her blouse in the tiny basin in the Blue Room (lavatory), the stewardess finished working her trip with her wet hair tied in a turban and wearing her winter coat.[59]

SAFETY AND EVACUATION

Safety was of prime importance for the stewardess, and instructions were given for emergencies, including the necessity of evacuating passengers as follows:

> Instruct passengers not to smoke; make sure the seat belts are securely fastened; instruct passengers to keep their heads braced

against the back of their seats; instruct passengers to brace their feet against something solid, with the knees bent slightly and the muscles tense; instruct passengers to remain seated until the plane comes to a complete stop or until they are advised that they may move; have passengers remove their glasses; give each passenger a pillow, in the event the plane noses over. This precaution is used to protect the face from bumping the seat ahead.

EMERGENCY EXITS

If the cabin entrance door jams, the emergency exits should be used.

When using the emergency exits, it is better to allow a couple of men passengers to leave first, so that they may be able to assist the women in getting down from the wing. As an extra precaution, ask the women with high heels to remove their shoes.[60]

SOME SPECIAL PASSENGERS

Stewardesses were often called upon to handle difficult situations with passengers, as illustrated by the following story:

In 1947 several groups of Basque shepherds were being hired by ranchers in the west to look after herds of sheep. It was a common practice to give two-year contracts to the Basque herders from Europe.

After the arrival of the Basques in the United States, they boarded a United DC-3 flight originating in Newark, New Jersey, which made every single stop on United's mainline route. The flight took more than 24 hours from Newark to Elko, Nevada, the herder's final destination. They spoke either French or Spanish and no English. Since they had trouble communicating they were told, "Do not get off the plane for any reason, until you reach Elko."

The flight attendant working on a route had four Basque herders among the 21 passengers. When the flight landed in Cheyenne, Wyoming, she was advised that the plane would be going into the DC-3 maintenance base in Cheyenne for a scheduled major overhaul. She informed the passengers they would be transferring to another DC-3 plane for the remainder of the trip. All the passengers deplaned, except the four Basque shepherds.

"Using my best sign language, I indicated to them that this airplane was going no further, but pointing to the other plane on the tarmac, that plane

was going to Elko," the stewardess explained. The Basques had been well coached and they refused to get off the plane until it reached Elko. All four of the Basque passengers sat with arms folded, heads lowered, and refused to move.

Eventually, the Captain stepped into the cabin to find out what was happening. The Captain pointed to each man and asked, "Elko?" Each man nodded in the affirmative. The Captain marched off the plane, shouting, "Elko," and the men all followed obediently, probably realizing they were not going anywhere on that plane if the Captain was leaving.[61]

MANAGEMENT TRAINING

United Air Lines continued to upgrade training for all employees. The company held a stewardess management conference in Cheyenne, Wyoming, September 11–13, 1951.

The conference topics included: purpose of the conference, training employees, maintaining service at a desired level, discipline, airline and stewardess agreements, passenger complaints, department organization, schedules and reports, informing employees, attitude, case studies, review and conclusions.

Passenger service objectives and stewardess responsibilities were outlined:

> To contact the public in a courteous, friendly, personalized manner.
> To please the patron with smooth, sure, and consistent procedures.
> To induce by our sincere, mature behavior a feeling of confidence and security.
> To avoid any confusion arousing uncertainty in the mind of the passenger.
> To provide adequately for his comfort and convenience.
> To complete each task without delays, disturbances, or errors in handling.
> To anticipate the desires of the public and to meet them to the greatest possible extent.[62]

The employment training section emphasized that training of employees must be consistent with company policy and embody company philosophy. It noted that good training reduces dissatisfaction, absenteeism and turnover because it helps both new and experienced employees to fully use their individual capacities.

The importance of the role of supervisor of stewardesses was stressed in the training conference. Discussion included maintaining enthusiasm and developing an attitude of high quality in service. Supervisors were reminded to make sure stewardesses retained a high level of enthusiasm by showing such traits by example, correction and personal contact. Methods of discipline were also discussed, keeping in mind that "people generally do not resent or oppose necessary rules and regulations, if the rules and regulations are clear and the reasons for their existence is understood."

The conference also included discussion and case studies about passenger complaints. It was noted that of the thousands of passengers who travel, only a few take the time to write to the company about service. Usually cases of either superior or inferior service were brought to the attention of management. Emphasis was given to taking immediate action to correct cases of substandard service.

Additional topics covered at the conference included filing reports, duties of supervisors and miscellaneous items. In conclusion, the conference objective was to improve the stewardess service of United Air Lines, and participants were urged to see that stewardess service was the best possible on every occasion.[63]

For another decade, United Air Lines stewardesses continued to be trained at the facility in Cheyenne, Wyoming. Various milestones were often celebrated throughout the years of service.

The twentieth birthday celebration of stewardess service was recognized in several cities, but the chief celebration was in Denver. Members of the stewardess training class in Cheyenne were flown to Denver to attend the party. United's president William "Pat" Patterson was in attendance to honor Ellen Church, the world's first sky girl, and Steve Stimpson, the man who hired Church.[64]

During the event, Janet Winkler, a student from the Cheyenne school, received her wings from Ellen Church. Winkler was honored as the 3,000th stewardess graduating from United Air Lines training. It was reported that 61 present-day and 56 former stewardesses attended the Denver event.[65]

A 1957 report from United Air Lines stated that during the first four months of the year, United flew a total of 2,856 passengers into and out of Cheyenne Municipal Airport. During the same period, company planes carried 18,528 pounds of freight, 4,791 pounds of mail and 8,480 pounds of express to and from the state capital. Responsibility for the education

Stewardesses pose on the boarding stairway of a plane at the United Air Lines training school in Cheyenne, Wyoming. *Wyoming State Archives, Department of State Parks and Cultural Resources.*

and training center was vested in T. Lee Jr. His aides were Jack Hayes, superintendent of management training; Tom Pierson, supervisor of stewardess training; and R.E. Parish, supervisor of field training.

The report also stated that 1,400 employees of United were scheduled to undergo various types of training in Cheyenne for periods of from one to five weeks during 1957. A total of 530 stewardesses received their training at the Cheyenne center in 1956, and 600 women were expected to be trained in 1957.[66]

More than six thousand stewardesses received diplomas from the Cheyenne facility during the fourteen years of its operation. Some were dubbed with the affectionate title of "Sky Girls." Many of these Sky Girls recorded memories of their experiences as both students and graduates. Some provided colorful accounts about events that happened when they applied their knowledge in providing passenger service.

4

The Early Sky Girls

ELLEN CHURCH

Ellen Church's journey began when she received her nursing degree at the University of Minnesota in 1926. After graduation, she served as a nurse in the French Hospital in San Francisco. One day, while on her way to the hospital, Ellen's journey took a different turn.

As she passed by the Boeing Air Transport office, she became intrigued with a sign promoting the new Boeing Model 80A passenger transport. She entered the office and struck up a conversation with the manager, Steve Stimpson. During the visit, the pair discussed the idea of hiring male stewards to attend to passengers on flights, and Church proposed the idea of hiring women instead.

When Ellen Church persuaded Boeing Air Transport to try out the idea of nurses as stewardesses in 1930, no one was quite sure how the idea would work out. It was a bold step, but the practical and persuasive young nurse who conceived of the daring idea did a sound job of selling her concept to the skeptical men of aviation.

Ellen Church helped select and train the first group of women, all nurses, who established a high standard of uniformity in the unique profession of stewardess. After a short training period in Cheyenne, Wyoming, Church took her first flight as a member of the flight crew on a Boeing 80A trimotor plane that carried twelve passengers at a speed of 120 miles an hour.

Early air patrons were delighted with the new service that featured young women caring for their needs high in the air, and it quickly captured

Ellen Church standing at the door of a United Air Lines plane, circa 1930s. *United Air Lines.*

the public's fancy. Church said, "We felt that registered nurses had the proper training for the kind of streamlined job which they were starting. They knew how to handle people. They understood discipline. They were taught to be resourceful."[67]

In the early days of the stewardess service, most pilots believed women had little business in an airliner flight crew. Ellen Church recalled an incident during one of her early flights: "The concern of the pilot was to fly his plane properly and to arrive at the destination as nearly on time as possible. On the flight I saw a woman passenger had become quite ill, and I diagnosed the woman's trouble as acute appendicitis." Church informed the pilot and told him that he should land at the next city so the woman could be taken to a hospital. The pilot "growled" at Church to give the woman a sedative and asserted that he could not make an unscheduled stop. Church was adamant and finally told the pilot that if he continued the flight, the woman's life would be in his hands. "That seemed to bother the pilot, so he radioed ahead to the next city for a doctor to come to the airport. When they landed and the doctor took charge of the passenger, he said that the woman did have appendicitis, very seriously, and that a delay might have been fatal." The pilot was quoted as saying, "Believe me, you will never hear another complaint out of me about stewardesses."[68]

After a year and a half as a stewardess, Ellen Church sustained an injury that ended her career. "I was not a stewardess nearly as long as I wanted to be," Ellen said. "An automobile accident, of all things, ended my career with United after just a year and a half. It left me with a shattered ankle, so I figured I'd go back to the University of Minnesota and get a little more education, specializing in pediatrics," she explained. She did return to the University of Minnesota for additional nursing training in pediatrics. In 1936, she joined the staff of the Milwaukee County Hospital as chief nurse of the children's department. A few years later, she became director of nurses at the Children's Hospital at Louisville, Kentucky.[69]

Like many of her fellow nurses, Ellen entered the Military Nurse Corps during World War II. She went overseas with the Army Nurse Corps and was awarded the Air Medal in 1944. She served in several different countries before being stationed in England, where she trained air evacuation nurses. These nurses were charged with the care of critically injured soldiers whose wounds could not be treated in the combat theater. Their skills saved many lives as the wounded were flown to the rear for more advanced medical attention. In her evacuation work, she often met former United Air Lines pilots who were flying DC-3 planes in and out of battle zones. Her friendship with the pilots was one of long standing, since she had known many of them on commercial flights while serving as the world's first air hostess.[70]

Following the war, Church served as administrator of the Union Hospital School of Nursing in Terre Haute, Indiana, from 1951 to 1964. She married Leonard Marshall in 1964.[71]

Ellen Church joined the military service during World War II. Lieutenant Church served as an air evacuation nurse of the Army Troop Carrier Command. *United Air Lines.*

During a radio interview on April 16, 1945, Ellen reminisced about her experiences as a stewardess and as a captain of the Army Nurse Corps–Air Evacuation Service. Of her service during World War II, she said, "I entered training at Bowman Field, Kentucky in 1942, and six weeks later found myself in Africa." From there, she was based in Sicily, Italy, and England. She was in England for D-Day and made numerous trips across the channel with sick and wounded soldiers. She recalled, "The soldiers expected so little that the least little thing we did for them seemed like something from heaven. They were marvelous, no complaints, no gripes, nothing but cooperation."[72]

Of the stewardess service she helped to launch, Church said, "It began as an experiment and survived only because we regarded it as a worthwhile service, demanding our best efforts. We knew that failure would extend beyond ourselves."[73]

Ellen Church Marshall died on August 27, 1965, after she was thrown from a horse. She is honored with a bronze statue and a plaque dedicated to her service as the world's first airline stewardess. United Air Lines dedicated the memorial at a ceremony in 1966 at United's Education and Training Center in Chicago.

The dedication on the plaque is inscribed:

World's First Airline Stewardess
Ellen Church Marshall
1904–1965

Humanitarian, war heroine and aviation pioneer, Ellen Church Marshall dedicated her indomitable spirit to the service of mankind.

As the world's first airline stewardess, she created a new and exciting profession for young girls of the 20th century.

As a much decorated Air Corps nurse in World War II, she brought comfort and relief to thousands of American soldiers who were wounded on the battlefields of Europe.

And as a peacetime nursing instructor and hospital administrator, she guided vast numbers of young women along the path once taken by another humanitarian, Florence Nightingale.

Born September 22, 1904 on a farm near Cresco, Iowa, Ellen Church Marshall combined imagination, persistence and her own personal warmth to meet life's challenges along the way; and with her death on August 27, 1965, the world lost a truly great and dedicated woman.

Her name will serve forever as the symbol of the selfless devotion that rests in the hearts of nurses and stewardesses all over the world.[74]

HARRIET FRY

Harriet Fry was one of the original eight stewardesses who flew into history by launching a career in the airline industry for young women. She was interviewed by Ellen Church in Chicago in 1930 and was accepted for training in Cheyenne, Wyoming, in early May.

Fry recalled that early stewardesses were required to perform many chores, including cleaning the plane's chemical toilets, hauling baggage and even helping refuel the plane. And when a plane broke down, sometimes landing in a cow pasture, the stewardess ended up babysitting the plane until mechanics arrived.

The position provided some glamour as well. "We had such pretty outfits," Harriet said. "The suits had green capes lined in gray silk. Someone called us 'the little green swallows.' It was so exciting when we swept onto the airstrip in Cheyenne, clad in our green capes, for our first official flight."[75]

There were many exciting trips for the original eight stewardesses who flew either a route from San Francisco to Cheyenne or a route from Cheyenne to Chicago. Fry described the Boeing 80-A plane she was assigned to:

> *Those biplanes were made of plywood and linen canvas. Every now and then a strip of canvas would work loose during flight and we had to make an emergency landing until we got the canvas glued back on. The planes were noisy, too. Before taking off, we gave each passenger some cotton batting to stuff in his ears and some tranquilizer to relax him. Most of our passengers were scared to death.*[76]

The plane that Fry flew on was a Boeing 80-A Trimotor. The plane consisted of a cockpit, mail pit, cabin and baggage compartment. The interior of the plane was made to look like the interior of a train coach. The seats were upholstered in gray fabric, and the seat could be reclined.

The original eight stewardesses, May 1930, Cheyenne, Wyoming. *Left to right*: Jessie Carter, Cornelia Peterman, Ellen Church, Inez Keller, Alva Johnson, Margaret Arnott, Ellis Crawford and Harriet Fry. *Wyoming State Archives, Department of State Parks and Cultural Resources.*

On the back of each seat was a pouch that contained a map, cards and a burp cup. Fry recalled, "Serving food and beverages was difficult because of the vibration of the plane, and there was often turbulence flying at altitudes from two to three thousand feet."[77]

She described the meals she served as containing fried chicken, bread and butter sandwiches, potato chips, pickles and olives, brandied fruit cocktail, tea, coffee or bouillon. The meals were served with china glasses, cups, saucers and plates and linen napkins. She said the china service was often broken because of rough weather and landings, so finally they were forced to use paper items.[78]

Fry told of often landing in a farmer's field, which sometimes made the farmers unhappy, especially when they discovered the planes were using hole-in-the-floor plumbing and garbage disposal. "We had to stop that and put in chemical toilets," she said. "But we were friends of the farmer, too, sometimes alerting them about a fire or other hazard on the farm."[79]

Harriet Fry resigned her stewardess position in August 1931 after flying for eighteen months, and she later married Howard Iden. "It was a great experience and I am glad I was one of the 'Original Eight.'"[80]

JESSIE CARTER

Jessie Carter was on hand for the fiftieth anniversary of the stewardess service 1980. She flew from her home in Hawaii to attend the festivities and reminisce about her days as one of the original eight stewardesses.

She recalled some of her exciting experiences: "I had never seen nor been on a plane or even been far from home. All of a sudden to be flying over the countryside and seeing a Model A and Model T Ford on the road below, well, it was a new world."[81]

Carter said she often felt lonely at first. She said she would sometimes see another stewardess while staying at the Plains Hotel in Cheyenne, Wyoming, but she never got to know any of the other women well. "The pilots ignored us, and a few wives of the pilots started a letter writing campaign to Boeing Air Transport administration objecting to us." Nevertheless, she continued to fly and enjoy new adventures.

She said she lost several boyfriends because of her job. "They would ask for a date and I would say, 'Well, I can't, tomorrow I have to fly to Cheyenne.' They would think I was making something up. People just didn't understand what we were doing. We didn't understand ourselves.

We just learned as we flew. When we took off we never knew when we would get back."[82]

As a stewardess, she recalled some of the duties she performed: "We were responsible for the food hamper with chicken, fruit cocktail, rolls, coffee and tea. We served coffee from a silver pot and served cold chicken on china plates. Big white napkins were spread across the passengers' laps. The silver service was quickly dented and those gorgeous china plates were often broken."[83]

The pilots were amazing and could really fly, Carter explained: "The pilots used telephone poles, railroad tracks, Rand McNally maps, towns or town's lights to guide them. There were no weather reports. Once you were in flight if you ran into a bad storm you either turned back or found a field closest to the nearest town. The delay could be four hours or two days."[84]

"The pilots knew every piece of ground that was big enough for an emergency landing from San Francisco to Chicago. One early morning the pilot made a beautiful landing in a field of sheep. The Captain, two passengers and I built a bonfire while we waited for the co-pilot to walk the four miles to the closest farmhouse. To us it was no big emergency," she recalled.[85]

Jessie Carter married L.E. Bronson, and like all stewardesses of her era, she had her "wings clipped" and had to retire from stewardess service.

INEZ KELLER

Inez Keller was a registered nurse living in San Francisco when she was recruited to fly for Boeing Air Transport in 1930. She flew on Boeing's Trimotor 80-A between San Francisco and Cheyenne.

Keller said the flight was supposed to take eighteen hours. Because of weather and the five stops along the route, the flight usually lasted up to twenty-four hours. If the twelve-passenger craft was fully loaded with passengers, the stewardess sat on the mail sacks or on a suitcase in the rear of the airplane. The planes were not pressurized, and they were cold and drafty.[86]

She also said the pilots were not enthusiastic about having women on the crew. "They were rugged characters who carried guns to protect the mail." However, the passengers appreciated the stewardess service, and the pilots came to grudgingly accept the women on the crew.[87]

"We wore our forest green wool suits with caps and a cape" before boarding the plane, Keller explained. "The cape had large pockets to hold a wrench, screwdriver, and a railroad timetable, all of which we used

The original eight stewardesses are shown in the top photo (*left to right*) Jessie Carter, Cornelia Peterman, Ellen Church, Inez Keller, Alva Johnson, Margaret Arnott, Ellis Crawford and Harriet Fry, In the bottom photo, five of the original eight stewardesses stand before a United Air Lines 747 christened *The Original Eight* in their honor at ceremonies on July 18, 1975, in Seattle. They are Jessie Carter Bronson, Cornelia Peterman Tyson, Inez Keller Fuite, Margaret Arnott and Harriet Fry Iden. *United Air Lines.*

frequently. But after boarding and while serving food to passengers we wore light gray nurse's uniforms and caps."[88]

There were strict requirements to become a stewardess, including the requirement that they could not weigh more than 115 pounds. Keller learned firsthand how weight affected the performance of the early planes: "The pilot couldn't gain enough altitude to fly over the mountains from Evanston, Wyoming, to Salt Lake City. So, he flew back to the airport and told me to get off."[89] Keller watched from below as the plane made it over the mountain seemingly because it was 115 pounds lighter.

Another time, the plane Keller was flying on ran out of gas and had to make an emergency landing in a wheat field in Wyoming. People from the surrounding area came in wagons and on horseback to see the plane. "They had never seen an aircraft before, and they wanted to touch it and to touch me. One of them called me 'the angel from the sky,'" she recalled.[90]

After she quit flying and married, Inez Keller Fuite concluded she had experienced some hair-raising events during her days as one of the first stewardesses.[91]

MARY O'CONNOR

Mary O'Connor was not one of the original eight stewardesses, but she joined the airline industry a few years later and became known as "the flyingest woman in the world." Mary logged seven million miles as a stewardess from 1933 to 1960.[92]

O'Connor said her friends thought flying was a pretty risky thing to do and not a safe way to make a living. She said the pilots were not open to accepting the stewardesses, but after the women brought the pilots a few cups of coffee and waited on them, they came to accept the stewardesses as a necessary evil.

Eventually, O'Connor became a stewardess trainer:

> *I would fly with the girls and watch them operate, then make suggestions. It was all on the job training, fun but difficult. Most of the girls I worked with or criticized were my good friends. The friendliness, the closeness and the togetherness of the crews and girls was unusual. It reached a point that our friends, who were not in aviation, were pretty bored with us. We talked about nothing but passengers and trips.*

Mary O'Connor posed in front of a United Air Lines plane named in her honor. O'Connor flew more than seven million miles while working for thirty-two years as a United stewardess. She was named United's chief stewardess for seven years and, during World War II, helped organize the navy's Air Evacuation Corps. *United Air Lines.*

One of the rewards of being a stewardess was the interesting people on the flights, according to O'Connor. She met Amelia Earhart, who encouraged her to learn to fly an airplane. She met Hollywood stars and politicians as well as regular passengers. She said the most interesting passenger was often the person who had never flown before. O'Connor also said the airline service was more personal in the early days, adding, "If we were ready to take off and a passenger called and said he'd be an hour late, we'd hold the plane for him."

After being passed over for a promotion to chief stewardess after working as a flight instructor for seven years, Mary O'Connor joined the navy and was stationed in Hawaii. She later served in Washington, D.C., teaching corpsmen and nurses evacuation techniques.

O'Connor rejoined the airlines in 1946. William Patterson, United Air Lines president, asked her to become his personal stewardess on his executive plane. She accepted and flew on the DC-3 named the *Mary O'Connor Mainliner*.

I ran it like a one woman airline. I set up the flights with dispatch; I organized the food service; I reserved the hotels. It was really great and I made the plane a flying hospitality center. The Executive Mainliner had a galley with an extra table for working and serving, and it had drawers for linens. The Pullman section could be converted into sleepers. There was a club room with comfortable chairs, a desk and a typewriter. We also rented the plane out to groups and organizations.[93]

Many famous people were guests aboard the *Mainliner O'Connor*. "On so many of the flights we had a party like spirit and such good times," she said. Former United Air Lines president Patterson praised O'Connor with these words: "She was always answering a fire alarm for others. When one of the employee's children was very ill, she flew to their aid. She was the Florence Nightingale of the air."[94]

Mary O'Connor summed up her career with the airlines with these words: "Up there the views are gorgeous, never the same any two days or any two hours. I never stayed long enough in one place to get married. My first love was flying and I'm still in love."[95]

LIBBY DOYLE

Beginning in 1942, many of the stewardesses who were nurses joined the military. They were needed to assist with many duties during World War II. To replenish the depleted stewardess ranks, United began accepting young women with a minimum of two years of college or a year of college combined with a year of business experience. However, the airline did not relax the rule about being unmarried.[96]

Libby Doyle was among the first who were not nurses to join the airlines. Her training included an extensive course in first aid from the Red Cross. She learned to bandage and unbandage, place broken bones in a splint and give artificial respiration. The stewardesses were instructed on the use of sleeping pills, aspirin, glass vials of ammonia and band-aids, all items that were included in their first-aid kits.

Doyle described other aspects of training: "We studied grooming, graceful movements, and a friendly smile. Our hair was short and above the collar. We wore knee length grey tailored suits in the winter and bright blue suits in the summer."[97]

She said they learned to serve food by giving the passenger a pillow to hold the food tray on their laps. She emphasized that no liquor was served because "alcohol in the system and a rough trip through cumulous clouds was a disastrous combination."

Libby flew between Chicago and Denver, Chicago and Cheyenne and Chicago and the East Coast. "It was a long and often rough trip from Chicago to Denver or Cheyenne," she said. Some of her most strenuous work involved lifting the food carriers over the partition of the luggage compartment in the tail of the airplane. "Sometimes I had to call the Captain for help when I just couldn't move the heavy stack of trays."

Since it was during the war, there were strict regulations.

No one was permitted to take photographs from the air. I had this gentleman on a trip who insisted on clicking away and he refused to give me the camera. One of the pilots came back and convinced him to relinquish his camera. We notified ground personnel who met him as he departed the plane. We never heard what happened, but I like to fantasize that we smashed a spy ring.

She also said that anytime the plane flew over a military installation or a coastal city the window curtains had to be drawn. "I flew over New York City for two years and never saw the city from the air until the blackout was lifted. I can still remember the beautiful sight of the city at night, lit up by a gigantic Christmas tree."

One of Libby Doyle's favorite aspects of being a stewardess was visiting with passengers. She said every individual was interesting and she could always find something to discuss. Since she was from a small town in Illinois, she felt she could relate well to passengers. "I think that small town girls have a different rapport with the passengers than a city girl, mainly because we knew everybody who lived in the small town where we grew up."

As with all stewardesses of her era, she was required to resign when she married. She expressed that she enjoyed her work very much and regretted leaving her days of adventure in the sky.[98]

Cheyenne's Sky Girl Graduates

MILDRED "MILLIE" STURDEVANT

Born into an aviation-minded family in 1921, Millie Sturdevant grew up hearing about pilots and airplanes. Two of her three brothers were pilots, and her brother Orville Foster Sturdevant was a chief pilot for United Air Lines.

Millie graduated from the University of Colorado in Boulder in 1945 and expected to apply to become a stewardess. Much to her disappointment, she found out she was two inches taller than the height limit at the time of five feet and five inches.

For a time, she worked for a Texas-based oil company as a statistician. As men returned from World War II, the company opted to give returning veterans jobs. Sturdevant trained five of the men in the accounting department. When one of the men was promoted to a job ahead of her, she went to the office of the company president to complain. When she told him that the promotion of one of her trainees to be her superior was a slam to her work, he disagreed. He told her, "You're a good-looking redhead. Soon you will be married and having kids." She resigned that day in July 1947.

Out of work, she wondered what she would do. Fortunately, very soon thereafter United lifted the height restrictions barring her from applying, and she immediately talked to her brother Orville. He thought it would be a good idea for her to become a stewardess, and he would "let" her, if he heard no rumors about her. Millie submitted her application and soon found herself in Cheyenne, Wyoming, as a student in one of the first classes offered at the newly relocated United Air Lines Stewardess Training Center.

The demand for new stewardesses was accelerating, and Sturdevant found herself in a training that would take only two weeks. "Cheyenne was a very small town, but I loved it. The clouds there were the prettiest I would ever see," she exclaimed.

Sturdevant has memories of living with six to eight other women in a room. There was a lot to be learned. She described the training to include learning how to deal with fire and evacuate planes by using the inflatable chutes. A plane was brought to the training center while undergoing maintenance for their instruction and practice. In the classrooms, she was also trained in how to deal with any other conceivable emergency from medical incidents to caring for infants. She also learned the history and the geography of all of United's routes so she could address points of interest. Included with the training was the use of the new "buffets," as stewardesses had to prepare the meals for passengers along the way. With a sharp mind, she also could learn the name of each passenger on her aircraft.

With such a short course, Sturdevant recalled there was little to do during the week but go to class during the day and study during the night. Trainees were not allowed to leave the airfield and took their meals at the cafeteria, a remnant of the facilities of the modification center. Even exercise was done on campus. Sturdevant said she and her classmates were so exhausted from the training that they did little more than talk in the evenings before retiring. On the weekends, however, they went to the Plains Hotel to relax and dance.

The graduation ceremony for Millie Sturdevant and her classmates was held in July 1947 at the cafeteria adjoining the Cheyenne training center. Each was issued a stewardess cap, and the ceremony included a brief introduction of each graduate before the pins were awarded. Sturdevant had hoped to be based in San Francisco but was instead sent back to Denver. The apartments where she lived did not allow single women, so she and her sister lived together. When her sister moved to San Francisco, another stewardess, Barbara Jean Jessup, moved in. Eventually, her brother Orville would end up marrying this new roommate.

On her first flight, she was assigned to a DC-3 with twenty-one passengers. As was tradition with all new stewardesses, Sturdevant was invited up to the cockpit. It was normal hazing to have the new stewardess sit on the pilot's lap. When she appeared, however, the crew recognized her. "Oh, you're Sturdy's sister." They never gave her any trouble after that. Not all went smoothly, however. On the DC-3, the stewardess jump seat used to be right by the door to the cockpit at the front of the plane. On one takeoff, the door to the outside sprang open right next to her while the plane taxied. She hurriedly used the intercom to alert the crew of the problem, and they aborted the takeoff. Instead of being heralded for her quick thinking, Sturdevant was berated. The irritated pilot explained that wind pressure would have stopped the door from opening the rest of the way, and she was warned never to cause trouble on a takeoff again. Another memorable experience happened while flying

Mildred "Millie" Sturdevant graduated from the United Air Lines Cheyenne Training Center in 1947. *Courtesy of Millie Sturdevant Fitzpatrick.*

over the Grand Canyon. Smoke poured through the air vents and started to fill the cabin. Apparently, there was no danger unless someone smoked. Fortunately, no one did, and the plane arrived safely in Denver.

Millie Sturdevant flew out of Denver until 1948. On a "turn-around" flight, a man sat next to her and introduced himself as the passenger service manager from United. He invited her to apply to work as the assistant chief stewardess for the Los Angeles domicile. She eagerly snapped up the opportunity and worked in that capacity until 1951.

She met several celebrities along the way. She flew frequently with Jimmy Stewart as well as the president of the University of Colorado. Ever outgoing, Sturdevant found herself doing several promotions for United's Mainliner flights from Los Angeles to New York and for United's routes to Hawaii.

She often returned to the Plains Hotel in Cheyenne for United Air Lines conferences. The senior stewardesses, chefs and United's executives met there twice a year.

Millie Sturdevant met and married her husband, Gilbert Fitzpatrick, in 1951, ending her stewardess career. The couple moved to Cleveland, and she continued to work for United Air Lines at the Cleveland airport for another nine years before transferring back to Denver. Because of her

Millie Sturdevant (*left*) packs her bag for her flight to a gala New Year's Eve party, while her roommate, Jean Kohnen, contemplates the fact that she will spend New Year's Eve on assignment aboard her flight. *Courtesy of Millie Sturdevant Fitzpatrick.*

outgoing personality and experience, she was a valuable asset to United and worked extensively with international passengers.

For her eightieth birthday, Millie's family gave her the opportunity to take a glider ride from the Colorado Springs airport. "When I saw that glider without an engine, I thought I will never get in that contraption, but

Right: Millie Sturdevant (*right*) celebrates with Albert Lino, Honolulu, Hawaii postmaster, on the occasion of jet airmail service delivery aboard United Air Lines to Hawaii. *Courtesy of Millie Sturdevant Fitzpatrick.*

Below: Millie Sturdevant (*kneeling*) examines the Hawaiian-themed fabric, modeled by an unidentified woman, in celebration of a flight aboard the United Air Lines Stratocruiser from Los Angeles to Honolulu in 1950. Millie still has the Hawaiian fabric draped around her neck that she received seventy years earlier. *Courtesy of Millie Sturdevant Fitzpatrick.*

I saw my family watching me, so I crawled in for an hour of one of the best adventures I have ever had," she said. "It was on par with the balloon ride I took in Africa, where we saw giraffes, elephants, gazelles and water buffalo while floating above the desert. When we landed a crew following on the ground set up a griddle to cook our breakfast, and we dined at a table with crystal dishes and drank champagne."

The ninety-eight-year-old former stewardess continues to live in Denver, where she is active in her community. She enjoys belonging to the Clipped Wings chapter, where she meets often with her fellow retired stewardesses. On a recent outing with friends who were recalling their memorable flights, Millie shared a story that brought laughter to the group. "I was flying back from Paris when the man in front of me reclined his seat. I said loudly enough for him to hear, 'If I'm going to have a man in my lap, I don't want a seat between us,' and without a word his seat went back to the upright position."

Millie has a million stories to tell about her years flying through a sky filled with the most beautiful clouds she has ever seen.[99]

JANE FORBES

Jane Forbes became interested in flying when she took an aviation course at her Hillsboro, Illinois high school in 1944. The course did not involve any flying but instead relied on books to teach the basics of flight. After graduation, Forbes took flight training at Stevens' Private College in Columbia, Missouri, graduating in 1948.

Serendipity provided Forbes with an opportunity to join the flight industry. She traveled to Boulder, Colorado, to join her boyfriend at a Phi Delta formal spring dance at the University of Colorado. While at the dance, Forbes met a friend who worked for United Air Lines. Upon his recommendation, she applied for stewardess school but learned that she was too young at the age of twenty to be accepted. Instead, she took a job working the payload control office in Denver, regulating the seating on flights.

A year later, Forbes was able to qualify for training and was accepted into the stewardess program in Cheyenne, Wyoming. She arrived in Cheyenne in 1949, just after the worst spring snowstorms the state had ever recorded, thinking it was the end of the world.

Like most other women who attended the program, Forbes found the following days of training a blur of activity. The training schedule consisted of classes for eight hours a day, five days a week, and included topics such

Candidates for stewardess training in Cheyenne, Wyoming, relax in their dormitory in this photo circa 1950s. *United Air Lines.*

as meteorology, communications and principles of aeronautics, infant care, graceful walking, flight connections and general geography. Additional courses included the history of the airline and the serving of in-flight meals and other duties.

A mockup of an airliner was located in an old hangar formerly used for aircraft maintenance. Using the simulator, instructors walked the candidates through every aspect of a typical flight, such as how to take care

This mock-up of the interior of a DC-6 Mainliner was used for instruction at the United Air Lines Stewardess School in Cheyenne, Wyoming, in 1953. Scotty Sinclair (*standing left*) demonstrates the correct form in handling a meal tray while Elizabeth Swartz prepares food set-ups in the aft galley. *United Air Lines.*

of passengers, how to learn their names, how to fasten seatbelts and how to train for emergencies. The trainees were required to wear suitable attire during training, including high heels, stockings, a girdle and a full slip.

The stewardesses were housed at a dormitory located at the training center. Conditions were Spartan and privacy almost nonexistent. Each room housed up to twenty stewardesses who each had a bed and a dresser. It was in the dormitory that most students took time to study, socialize and relax. In their leisure time on weekends, the classmates visited local restaurants and bars. A favorite place that Jane Forbes recalled was the Little Bear Inn north of Cheyenne. Another frequented place was the Wigwam Lounge in the Plains Hotel. The women often met the young men of the town who showed up at the Plains Hotel at just the right time.

Near the conclusion of training, the candidates enjoyed a brief flight on an airliner. Forbes remembered that her flight consisted of a quick passage over

Cheyenne and down to Denver. The classmates participated in graduation ceremonies in Denver.

Forbes began her nearly three-year career with United Air Lines and recalled some of her experiences. "We were responsible for the comfort of the passengers, including when the plane went through turbulence or when a passenger became ill. I remember helping a passenger use the 'burp cup' on a rough flight to Chicago. A passenger who became ill and used the burp cup also lost his false teeth in the burp cup. There was nothing I could do but to fish them out."

After serving as a stewardess, Forbes was asked to become an instructor at the Cheyenne training facility in May 1952. She enjoyed teaching the new classes until she had to resign after her marriage in November 1952.

While requirements came and went with the changing demands of the airline, marriage was still the end of a stewardess's career until it was ruled in 1970 to be in violation of the Civil Rights Act of 1964. Former stewardesses were allowed to return to work if they chose to do so, but Jane Forbes declined to return to her previous career as a stewardess and an instructor.[100]

SUSAN DITTMAN

A former stewardess and friend of Jane Forbes recalled her most memorable odd flight:

> We had a trip from Chicago to Boston with a stop in Hartford, Connecticut. We had about 30 passengers from the Hartford station. One of those passengers, a woman about 75 years old, was sitting in the first row of a DC-6 with no one next to her. As the door was closed she began to become somewhat violent and wanted out of there and was very confused, so we got her strapped down and I had to hold the seat belt end so that she wouldn't get up. She was almost uncontrollable.
>
> I thought she would react quietly to a Catholic priest since she had a good Catholic name, but she hit at the priest and broke his glasses. Then I thought a glass of water would have a calming effect and she threw it at me. Little did I know the water made my mascara run and I looked as if I had a black eye.
>
> This event went on for the 45 minutes it took to get to Boston. The pilots radioed ahead for her family and after everyone else deplaned her family came on board. Then she became very rational and turned to me and said as

sweet as possible, "Thank you dear." The ground crew thought I had been beaten up. I hadn't, just the mascara running down my face.

Another passenger sent a letter about us to UAL saying how good we were to her. I can still see her, especially saying, "Thank you dear."[101]

ALDA KESSLER

Life on a remote ranch in southeastern Wyoming might lead to a young woman dreaming of flying through the bright blue skies to more exotic destinations. Such dreams were realized for one resident of LaGrange, Wyoming.

Alda Kessler attended a one-room elementary school near her family's ranch with eight other pupils. She went on to graduate from LaGrange High School along with five classmates and then to graduate from the University of Wyoming in 1950.

The Wyoming native's plans to become a teacher were suddenly changed when Kessler decided to apply to attend the United Air Lines Stewardess Training Facility in Cheyenne, Wyoming. "I thought it sounded like fun, I wanted to fly, and it seemed like it would be a way to have a paid vacation," she recalled.

"I was so anxious to be admitted to the training program," Kessler said, "that I exaggerated the size of our ranch, telling the interviewer it was larger than it really was. I thought that may have impressed the person conducting the interview." She anxiously waited for an answer and was so excited when she learned she had been accepted.

"The five-week program began when I moved into the dormitory at the training facility at the Cheyenne airport along with twenty-three other students. I was five foot, three inches tall and weighed 123 pounds. We had to dress up each day and wear nylon stockings with a seam in the back, and that seam had to be straight," she said.

Some things she remembers about the training classes were memorizing every state, where it was located and the capital of each state, along with safety procedures. Kessler said her group sometimes went out to dinner together, but most of the time was spent studying. "I took some of my friends to visit at the ranch near LaGrange for a weekend," she added.

Alda Kessler's class graduated on May 1, 1951. "I was the only one who cried at graduation because I wanted to be stationed in Denver, but I was sent to Los Angeles instead. But it worked out alright because it was the first time I saw the ocean or palm trees."

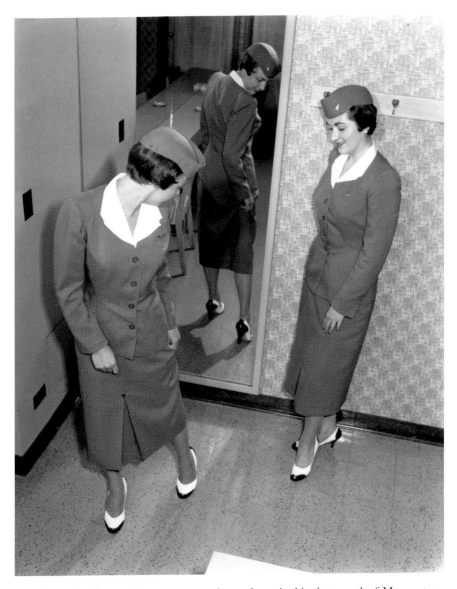

The dress code of stewardesses was very strict, as shown in this photograph of Margaret Mongeau checking the seam in her nylon stockings. Beverly Chappell (*right*), stewardess counselor for United Air Lines, watches to see if the hosiery seams are straight and the hemline is the prescribed length. *United Air Lines.*

Alda Kessler graduated in 1951 from the Cheyenne Stewardess School. She is shown here in the middle row, second from the right. Jean Allman, sitting to the right of Alda, became Alda's best friend and sister-in-law. Another classmate is Eve Tidalti, fifth from the left in the front row. *Courtesy of Alda Kessler Stewart.*

"I loved what I did and meeting the people," Kessler said. "We had no problems with security at that time. The food we served was wonderful. We had time to sit down and visit with the passengers. The worst problem was when we had rough weather that made people sick including the stewardess," she related.

The plane that Kessler flew on and enjoyed the most was the DC-6. Her route included flying from Los Angeles to the cities of Seattle, Chicago, San Francisco, Sacramento, San Diego and Catalina Island. She disliked the route to Sacramento because it was like a "milk run" that stopped at several little towns along the way.

One of her favorite memories from her career as a stewardess included meeting a famous Hollywood actor. "I was on a charter flight with Jimmy Stewart, his wife and a crew of twelve on a flight to Reno, Nevada. Photographers met the plane and took a publicity photo of Jimmy Stewart

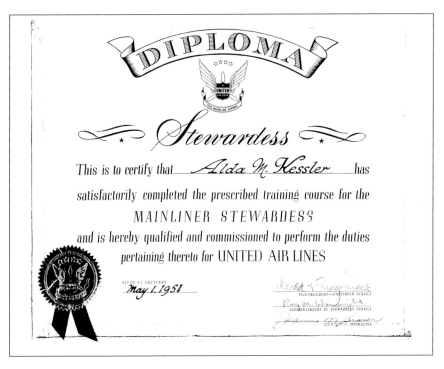

"Westerner" Jimmie Stewart shows stewardess Alta Kessler how to handle gun.

Above: Alda Kessler received her United Air Lines diploma at a ceremony in Denver, Colorado, after graduating from the Cheyenne Training Center on May 1, 1951. *Courtesy of Alda Kessler Stewart.*

Left: The actor Jimmy Stewart showing stewardess Alda Kessler the proper way to hold a gun in a promotional photograph at Reno, Nevada, in 1952. The photo appeared in the August 1952 issue of *Silver Screen* magazine. Kessler was assigned to accompany Stewart's charter flight from California to Reno. *Courtesy of Alda Kessler Stewart.*

showing me how to hold a gun. I believe the gun was a movie prop provided just for the photo. I found out later the photo appeared in the August 1952 issue of *Silver Screen* movie magazine." Kessler said that sometimes on a day off the airline would call to see if a stewardess was available for a last-minute charter flight. "That was my lucky day," she added.

Like many of the stewardesses in the 1950s, Alda Kessler worked for one year before leaving her profession. At that time, it was required that she had to leave work when she married.

> *My best friend from the training school, Nelda Allman, introduced me to her brother, Dale Allman, and we married in 1952. We had a little boy, and I was pregnant with twins when Dale died after three years of marriage. Nelda also introduced me to my second husband, Jerry Stewart. He had four boys, I had three children, and we had two more children, so we raised nine children. I have twenty-five grandchildren and at least thirty great-grandchildren.*

Another favorite memory of her days as a stewardess was receiving "letters from passengers thanking us for our service." One such letter bearing the letterhead "An Orchid to You" contained the following message:

> *Our recent itinerary included a visit to L.A. from Sacramento. We went aboard United's Flight 278 and while it was a short flight it was most interesting because of the excellent manner in which our needs were served by your very efficient "hostess" Miss Kessler. She was capable, gracious and sincere in her attempts to make each passenger enjoy his trip. It was a pleasure to have been aboard.*

The letter writer received a response from management stating in part, "It was thoughtful of you to tell me how much stewardess Alda Kessler helped to make your recent flight from Sacramento to Los Angeles so pleasant and enjoyable. I hope that your future flights along the Main Line will be as pleasant as this one; if I can ever offer a personal assistance with your travel problems, please let me know."

"Orchid Letters" are among Alda Kessler's most precious mementos from her days flying through that bright blue sky of her youthful dreams.[102]

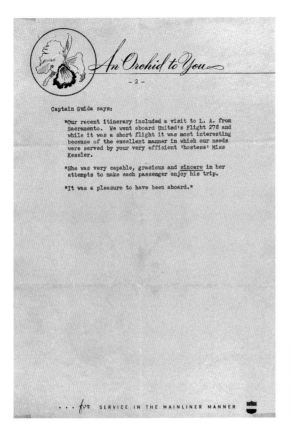

An Orchid to You
- 2 -

Captain Guida says:

"Our recent itinerary included a visit to L. A. from Sacramento. We went aboard United's Flight 278 and while it was a short flight it was most interesting because of the excellent manner in which our needs were served by your very efficient 'hostess' Miss Kessler.

"She was very capable, gracious and sincere in her attempts to make each passenger enjoy his trip.

"It was a pleasure to have been aboard."

... for SERVICE IN THE MAINLINER MANNER

Stewardesses often received Orchid Letters thanking them for their service. This letter was sent to Alda Kessler by one of her passengers. *Courtesy of Alda Kessler Stewart.*

PATRICIA "PATTY" SEIBEL

A career in music and teaching for Patricia "Patty" Seibel was soon replaced by an "itch to travel" and the realization that she didn't find teaching rewarding. After a semester teaching in Portland, Oregon, Seibel flew home to Centralia, Illinois, for Christmas. It was her first time flying, and she was curious about the role of the stewardess on the plane.

Patty Seibel had attended MacMurray College for Women for two years, but during a summer vacation, she had worked as a swimming instructor in Colorado. She liked Colorado, transferred to the University of Colorado and graduated in 1950 with a degree in music education. She accepted a job in Portland, where she taught 46 sixth graders, instructed 450 music students, attended night school, sang in a church choir and worked at a shoe store on Saturday. Seibel said it was the hardest job she ever had, and she felt that she was not suited to be a teacher.

On the flight home for Christmas, she observed the stewardess serving coffee, decided it looked like fun and asked the stewardess how she got her job. The next June, after declining to sign on for another year of teaching, Seibel stopped in Denver while she was on her way home by bus to Illinois. She interviewed with United Air Lines to train to become a stewardess. She received a letter of acceptance and reported to Cheyenne, Wyoming, in July 1951 for five weeks of training.

Twenty-three-year-old Patty Seibel joined ten other women at the United Air Lines Training Center located at the airport in Cheyenne, which she described as being "the middle of nowhere." They were housed in a two-story brick dormitory that also included classrooms and a cafeteria, she said.

Patricia Seibel graduated from the Cheyenne Training Facility in 1951 and is shown here wearing her United Air Lines hat and pin. *Courtesy of Patricia Seibel Romeo.*

From the very first day we were drilled on punctuality. We wore dresses, stockings and heels almost every day, with a few exceptions. Classes lasted all day where we learned safety procedures, what to do in an emergency, and the importance of serving a meal. It was also made clear that we were representatives of the airline, and being attractive, well-educated and outgoing were important qualifications.

The women were trained by a stewardess named Sally who came to Cheyenne to lead the class and was still a working stewardess. "We all adored Sally and thought she was the prettiest one among us."

At the end of training each day, the women were allowed to visit downtown Cheyenne for a few hours. "Our chauffeur was an old bow-legged cowboy in boots and a Stetson hat, who drove a station wagon to take us downtown," Seibel related. They sometimes went to the Lariat Lounge at the Frontier Hotel, but the most famous gathering place was the Wigwam Lounge at the Plains Hotel on Central and Sixteenth Avenues. The women were usually dropped off on Capitol Avenue, one block west of Central. They would then walk through an alley to enter

One of the instructors at the United Air Lines Training Facility in Cheyenne was this woman, named Sally. Her last name is unknown, but she was a favorite of the class that graduated in July 1951. *Courtesy of Patricia Seibel Romeo.*

the Plains Hotel. The alley became known as "Peacock Alley," because of the pretty girls parading through. Somehow, the young men of the town were waiting just inside the door of the Plains Hotel to greet the stewardesses.

Seibel said that shortly after her group began school, a group of Air Force Reserve pilots arrived on base, which was located at the Cheyenne airport. They had been activated for training and ate in the same cafeteria as the stewardesses. "Life became more interesting after the arrival of the men but proved to be a disaster for one of our classmates. She arrived fifteen minutes after our 10:00 p.m. curfew one night and was promptly dismissed and sent home."

The group then consisted of ten women. At the end of the third week of training, the students received their hats and were measured for uniforms. There were strict requirements for height and weight and only two sizes of uniforms were available, ten and twelve. Near the end of the five-week class, bids were accepted for the routes the stewardesses would fly. Four of the women in Patty Seibel's class had become good friends and secured a bid to be stationed in Los Angeles.

Patricia Seibel, second from right in white shirt, and classmates take time for some fun during a break in classes at Cheyenne in 1951. *Courtesy of Patricia Seibel Romeo.*

Graduation ceremonies were held in Denver at the Cosmopolitan Hotel. The soon-to-be graduates rode the bus to Denver except for one member of the class, who had never flown before, so she was flown to Denver so that her first assignment as a stewardess would not be her first flight, Seibel explained.

"After a lovely lunch, the president of United Air Lines, William Patterson, handed us our diplomas and pinned on our wings. It felt very special that Mr. Patterson would come all the way from Chicago to attend a graduation for ten women," she said. The new graduates were given airline passes and two weeks of free time before reporting for duty. "I felt like a princess as I went to the airport wearing my new light blue summer uniform, but I soon discovered the reality of flying 'stand-by.' I waited for hours to gain a seat. I only had twenty-four hours of seniority, so much for being a princess," Seibel said with a laugh.

Two weeks later, the four friends, Patty, Norma, Mary and Suzy, rented a house in Los Angeles together, bought a car and began their careers as stewardesses. Patty was assigned to fly a route from Los Angeles to San Francisco.

The pilots on Seibel's route referred to the flight as the "Valley Queen." Flying on a DC-3 airplane were the pilot, a co-pilot and one stewardess with a capacity for twenty-one passengers. The flight began in Los Angeles, stopped at Bakersfield, Visalia, Fresno, Merced and Modesto and ended in

This July 1951 class of stewardesses posed in their new caps in front of the United Air Lines Cheyenne Training Facility. *Front row, left to right*: Patricia Seibel, unidentified, Mary Morris, Susie Huggins. In the back row, fourth from left is Norma Hale, others unidentified. *Courtesy of Patricia Seibel Romeo.*

San Francisco. A meal had to be served on each segment of the flight, which kept the stewardess very busy.

Patty developed a routine for saving time when meals were served on a flight. Before the plane left the airfield, she removed the covers from the trays of food that contained the salad and other cold portions of the meal. Then they were stacked on a cart and stored in what was called the "blue room," to keep them cold. She kept the hot portion of the meal separate so it could be heated; then the cold trays were pulled from the blue room and served efficiently and quickly. The blue room was actually the restroom, and there

Above: The graduating class of July 1951 from the Cheyenne school, during ceremonies in Denver, Colorado. *Front row, from left*: unidentified, Susie Huggins, instructor Sally, Patricia Seibel and Norma Hale. In the back row, second from left is Mary Morris; others are unidentified. *Courtesy of Patricia Seibel Romeo.*

Right: Patricia Seibel and her best friend, Norma Hale, posed for a photo following graduation from the Cheyenne Training Center in 1951. *Courtesy of Patricia Seibel Romeo.*

was only one on the plane. "It worked well until one day, as the flight took off, there was a little turbulence and the cart with trays in the blue room shifted. The cart wedged up against the door handle and I couldn't get the door open. I asked the co-pilot for help, he had to get a screw driver and remove the door completely. By then we were ready to land and no one had received a meal," Seibel recalled with a laugh.

Another accommodation on the Valley Queen was a compartment behind the cockpit that was often used to transport agricultural products. "One item was strawberries, which had an unpleasant odor after a few hours on the plane. We also sometimes carried baby chickens and even dogs, but the service was finally discontinued to our relief," Seibel related.

> *An important part of our job was to welcome the passengers and make sure they were comfortable. Most people had never flown before and were often frightened. I sometimes sat down with a passenger and talked with them to ease their worries. Sometimes, a passenger would be traveling to a funeral and needed some sympathy. I became acquainted with the many traveling salesmen who rode the Valley Queen. They often got off at the first town on the route, and the next day boarded again for the next town. A pickle salesman who travelled the entire route stopping at each town along the way gave me a case of pickles one time.*

The stewardesses and pilots became acquainted, and friendships and relationships were developed. The pilots enjoyed teasing the stewardesses and pulling pranks on them. Mary was the youngest and most naive of Patty Seibel's stewardess friends and roommates, so the pilots liked to tease her. The DC-3 had a lever on the floor near the co-pilot that controlled the hydraulics. It often began to rattle, but by pushing the lever gently back and forth the rattle would stop. One day when Mary delivered coffee to the pilots, she asked what they were doing when they moved the lever back and forth. They told her it flushed the blue room and asked if she wanted to try it. She did, and then every so often they would ask her to flush the blue room again. When the pilots landed, they told the crew on the next flight what they had done and to continue the prank. Mary learned the truth a month later when a pilot who was not familiar with the prank yelled at her, "What are you doing?" when she tried to move the lever.

"Even though the pilots liked to tease us, we always felt we could rely on them. If anything ever went wrong, we could ask the pilot for help," Seibel said. One time she had been thrown to the floor during turbulence, and the

These women, who became close friends, were assigned to duty in Los Angeles, California, following training in Cheyenne, Wyoming. Pictured on the stairs of a DC-6 in the front row are Norma Hale (*left*) of Richmond, Indiana, and Suzy Huggins of Salem, Oregon. Back row are Mary Morse (*left*) of Espanola, New Mexico, and Pat Seibel of Centralia, Illinois. *Courtesy of Patricia Seibel Romeo.*

pilot "calmed me down and helped me to recover and finish my duties in the cabin, where one poor passenger had Thousand Island dressing all over her hair and clothing."

Seibel discovered there was one unmarried pilot she found attractive named Tony Romeo. Early in her career, she had been teasingly encouraged to sit on his lap in the cockpit before take-off, to which she complied, believing it was a good-natured joke. Patty and Tony were both stationed in Los Angeles, and they both loved music and the mountains of Colorado. Romeo grew up in Colorado, studied music and played the violin with the Colorado Symphony. However, World War II intervened, and he was drafted and became a navy pilot. After the war, he signed on with United Air Lines, where he served from 1951 to 1982. Following his training with United, he requested to be stationed in Denver. However, a fellow trainee who was married with children asked Romeo if he would trade for the Los Angeles route so he could remain in Denver. The pilots made very little money at the time, and the other man felt he could not afford to move and live in California. Tony Romeo agreed to take the Los

Angeles route, and it changed his life, of course, because that is where he met Patty Seibel.

The two dated for the next year and coped with the hectic schedules of working for the airlines. Tony was still flying out of California, but Patty had transferred to Denver, where she enjoyed meeting and socializing with Tony's sisters. "On one flight to Denver I was very tired," Tony said. "I went to bed at the Cosmopolitan Hotel and a half hour later the phone rang, it was Patty wanting to go to the mountains, so off we went. Later that night I flew back to Los Angeles," Tony explained. "By the next morning I had little sleep, was exhausted, and went to bed. Soon the phone rang and it was Patty telling me she had traded flights and was in Los Angeles. She wanted to go to the beach, so we did. Finally I decided I had two choices, marry Patty or die," Tony said with a twinkle in his eyes.

Patty and Tony married on December 28, 1952, in Illinois. They lived in Denver for five years, then in Boston and Chicago, eventually returning to Denver.

According to the airline rules at that time, Patty could no longer be a stewardess after marriage. She gave up flying and turned in her wings. She said she loved being a stewardess but was not disappointed at having to leave her career because she did want to marry and have a family. "And besides, I married a pilot, so I still was able to fly, and later on we took many flights with our children," Patty said. The Romeos had four children: Gina, Jeffrey, Julia and Chandler. Patty said she loved to cook and bake. She also liked to sew and made many of her own clothes and clothes for the children. She also returned to participating in music, joined a choir and performed soprano solos.

Patty remained active in the flight attendant community and was a member of Clipped Wings. The organization was formed in 1941 by former stewardess Jackie Jos Ceaser as a way to maintain her airline friendships and to participate in service to others. The name of the group came from the policy that when a young woman got married, she had to give up both flying and her wings: therefore, her wings were "clipped." Today the organization has thousands of members throughout the country with numerous local chapters. The members enjoy socializing and participating in community service.

Tony Romeo's career as a pilot includes many colorful stories as well. He was a flight instructor in Lander and Rock Springs, Wyoming. He flew many flights through Cheyenne, Rock Springs, Salt Lake City and around the West in the DC-3, DC-4 and the Convair 340 and 440. In October 1955, he

Stewardess Patricia Seibel and pilot Tony Romeo were married in 1953. They met while flying for United Air Lines. The couple resides in Denver, Colorado. *Starley Talbott photo.*

was asked to conduct an investigation of the United DC-4 that crashed into Medicine Bow Peak in Wyoming. In 1957, he transferred to Boston, and in 1960, he transferred to Chicago, where he became a captain. After retiring in 1982, he returned to Denver and was active in the community, including volunteering at the Wings Over the Rockies museum.

The Romeos enjoy retirement, family, community activities and travel. At age ninety-seven for Tony and age ninety-one for Patty, in 2019, they love to tell about their days "flying high in the sky."[103]

PHYLLIS JACK

Every Thursday, Phyllis Jack joins some her fellow retired stewardesses and other aviation volunteers at the United Air Lines Historical Foundation archives in Denver, Colorado. The volunteers work one day a week to preserve some of the records and artifacts related to the history of United Air Lines.

Phyllis Jack grew up in Cheyenne, Wyoming. After graduating from high school, she graduated from Iowa State University in 1952. She didn't find a job after college graduation, so she returned to Cheyenne to live with her parents, Huldah and William "Scotty" Jack. Her father served as Wyoming state auditor and secretary of state.

"I was doing odd jobs and becoming a pain in my father's side," Phyllis said. "One weekend I visited a high school friend in Denver who was working for an airline. Her roommate was a stewardess with United Air Lines. She regaled me with stories of how much fun it was to fly, so I thought it sounded like a fun job. I went home and told my dad about my possible interest in becoming a stewardess, but I didn't take any action," she related.

Not long after that, Phyllis took her place at the breakfast table where she was greeted with an application from United Air Lines to apply for training at the Cheyenne Stewardess Training Center. "Dad had gone to the center to pick up the application. So I filled it out and went to Denver for an interview. A few weeks later I moved into the dormitory with nine other young women at the Cheyenne airfield and began a five-and-a-half-week course to become a stewardess."

The ten young women in Phyllis's class shared a dormitory room on the second floor of the training center. Each woman had a bed, a dresser and a small locker that served as a closet. The dormitory room was on the window side of the building, and on the other side of the building were the classrooms.

Our housemother was called "Mom Thompson" and she was outgoing, compassionate and wonderful. We had a curfew and had to check in with her each night. Our days were filled with instructions on emergency situations, food service, and general passenger service. We stayed home during the weeknights and studied in our dorm room. Each morning we were tested on what we had learned the previous day. On the weekends we were taken by bus to downtown Cheyenne. We often went to the Wigwam Lounge at the Plains Hotel where we met friends and danced.

She also recalled that she had to memorize the route map across the United States and learn the three-letter codes for each city on the route. Following graduation in 1953, Phyllis was assigned to duty in Salt Lake City, where she served as a stewardess for one year. Her route usually consisted of stops in Twin Falls, Idaho, and Pendleton, Oregon, and ended at Portland, Oregon.

She had the urge to see more of the states, so she transferred to New York, where she flew on a DC-6 airplane. However, her time in New York was short-lived because the city was "not meant for this country girl," Phyllis said with a laugh. Then she transferred to Denver and worked a year from that domicile.

The following year, Phyllis had an opportunity to move to San Francisco and receive special training to fly the route to Hawaii on a DC-6 airplane. To fly that route, a stewardess had to have special training for over-the-water qualification. She found it very exciting to fly from San Francisco to Honolulu.

Because she had the proper qualifications and an international passport, Phillis signed on to fly military transports to Vietnam carrying military personnel back and forth from Travis Air Force Base in California. She also flew military transports to Frankfurt, Germany.

During the same period, Phyllis was recruited to teach stewardess classes back in Cheyenne. She conducted two short-term classes for three months each in 1957 and 1960. She taught the new trainees about the route map, emergency equipment, meal service and responsibilities toward passengers. "I found it very helpful to be able to teach the new women what I had learned by being a working stewardess," Phyllis said.

Following her teaching duties, Phyllis went back to flying and was stationed for a time in Washington, D.C., which she liked much better than New York. After a year seeing the sights around Washington, she returned to Denver, where she was requested to serve as a supervisor for stewardess service. "That job required a lot of paperwork. I worked on assigning routes, did check rides and desk duty on weekends. The check rides consisted of flying on a plane where other stewardesses were working and assessing their capabilities," Phyllis related. "While I was working in stewardess service, the stewardess union had negotiated a new contract that increased the base pay for working as a stewardess. So I went back to flying because I could make more money," she said.

United Air Lines had purchased the Pacific route from Pan Am, which provided Phyllis with some interesting opportunities to fly international. She flew from San Francisco to Tokyo and Hong Kong. Flying from Seattle to Japan proved to be very interesting, along with flying from Los Angeles to Hong Kong and Seoul. "However, my favorite country to visit was Australia," Phillis related. "We went on many day tours after landing in Sydney, and the people were so friendly and welcoming, and the country was so interesting," she said.

Retired airline stewardess Phyllis Jack poses with a uniform designed for the original eight stewardesses in 1930. The uniform is in the collection of the United Air Lines Foundation in Denver, Colorado, where Phyllis Jack volunteers. *Starley Talbott photo.*

Phyllis Jack was honored with a retirement party in 1998 by a group of her fellow stewardesses. Shown in front of a DC-3 airplane rented for a flight to commemorate the occasion are *(from left to right)* Diane Alder, Joyce Jeppesen and Phyllis Jack. *Courtesy of Bonita Ades.*

Phyllis flew for thirteen years on international flights, all the while living in Denver and commuting to the cities where the flights originated. Her last flight was to Hong Kong in the mid-1990s. She hurt her back in a non-work accident and underwent back surgery. Following her sick leave, she found herself unable to return to work, leading to her retirement after serving for forty-five years as a United Air Lines stewardess.

In May 1998, a group of stewardesses gave Phyllis Jack a retirement party to remember. They rented a DC-3 airplane at the Centennial, Colorado airport to fly around the Denver area for an hour. After the flight, they gathered at her home to celebrate her retirement with a catered brunch.

"I've had an exciting life flying all over the world," said the eighty-nine-year-old with a twinkle in her pretty blue eyes.[104]

CAROL UNTERBERG

When Carol Unterberg was eight years old, she ate a meal at a café overlooking Chicago's Midway Airport. Most of her food was untouched because she was fascinated by the airplanes flying in and out of the field. She expressed that someday she wanted to be a stewardess.

Unterberg began her journey to fulfill her dreams when she left Chicago to attend the United Air Lines Stewardess School in Cheyenne, Wyoming, in 1958. She had attended college at DePauw University and worked in the United Air Lines accounting department prior to being accepted for stewardess training.

"There was a lot more to being a stewardess than I had ever realized," Unterberg said. "The school was a lot like college including living in a dormitory, studying, and making friends," she explained.

Unterberg fit right into the Wyoming lifestyle by donning western clothing and participating in the annual Cheyenne Frontier Days celebration. She joined with her new friends in visiting local places, including the Little Bear Inn and the Wigwam Lounge at the Plains Hotel. She sometimes went on a date with a man who was based at nearby F.E. Warren Air Force Base.

The five weeks of training quickly flew by, and Unterberg and fifteen of her classmates attended formal graduation ceremonies in Denver. The women received their diplomas and wings from O.C. Enge, vice president of United Air Lines passenger service.

Enge expressed his interest in attending graduation for the stewardesses by saying, "You always know you're placing a large part of the company's

Stewardesses put in long hours of study time during training at the Cheyenne school. Shown here is Carol Unterberg during study time in 1958. *United Air Lines.*

reputation for service and courtesy in their hands. It's a great responsibility. I can't think of a finer group to do the job."

Even though Unterberg had hoped to be assigned to work in Chicago, she was assigned to Salt Lake City. "Becoming a stewardess is a dream come true, and I hope I will be wearing my wings when jet service is slated to begin in 1959," said the newly minted United Air Lines stewardess.[105]

Above: Carol Unterberg, stewardess in training, participated in the annual Cheyenne Frontier Days celebration by donning a cowgirl hat. *United Air Lines.*

Left: All decked out for Cheyenne Frontier Days is Carol Unterberg in a new pair of cowgirl boots while taking a break from attending stewardess training. *United Air Lines.*

A United Air Lines instructor (*left*) shows trainee Carol Unterberg a model of the interior of an airliner during training in Cheyenne. *United Air Lines.*

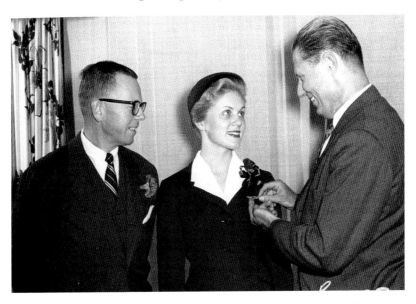

Carol Unterberg's newly won silver wings were admired by her father (*right*) on graduation day. O.C. Enge, vice president of passenger service, was present to congratulate Unterberg. *United Air Lines.*

EILEEN KITAGAWA

In honor of statehood for Hawaii, United Air Lines recruited candidates from the Hawaiian Islands for stewardess training. Eight young women were hired in 1960 and flown to the mainland for training.

Eileen Kitagawa flew five thousand miles from her home in Hawaii to join her classmates. Her flight took her to Los Angeles, then to Denver and finally to Cheyenne, Wyoming, where the training facility was located.

Kitagawa had been informed that there were four other women on her flight who were also headed to training in Cheyenne. She had brought along some leis, so she identified the other candidates and placed a lei around each of their necks. By giving the lei, a traditional Hawaiian greeting of welcome, Eileen began a friendship that was lasting. "We talked all the way to Cheyenne and were roommates during our training," she said.

Hawaiian-born Eileen Kitagawa (*right*) learned proper meal service techniques at the United Air Lines Stewardess Training School at Cheyenne, Wyoming. Mockups of cabin interiors enabled training in food service, ticketing and other in-flight procedures. *United Air Lines.*

Above: A group of stewardesses takes time out from training to enjoy outdoor activities available in Wyoming while attending classes in Cheyenne. These candidates *(from left to right)*, Patricia Keenan, Nancy Hoffman, Sylvia Montgomery and Scotty Sinclair, are headed for nearby snow-covered ski slopes. *United Air Lines.*

Left: Eileen Kitagawa received her wings at graduation in 1960. Tommy Dawson, superintendent of stewardess service at the United Air Lines training school in Cheyenne, Wyoming, pinned her wings to her uniform. *United Air Lines.*

Until the Boeing Stratocruiser went online, there was no plane that could fly from the mainland to Hawaii, about three thousand miles. Patricia Seibel (*right*) performed promotional work for United Air Lines and was chosen to meet this flight carrying Hilo Hattie and the first delivery of Hawaiian flowers to the mainland in April 1952. *Courtesy of Patricia Seibel Romeo.*

Like hundreds of students who had been trained in Cheyenne, Eileen and her classmates attended classes from 8:00 a.m. to 5:00 p.m. for five days each week. Their five weeks of education included food service, meteorology, aerodynamics, geography, charm and grooming, ticketing and airline routes and codes.

Sometimes the trainees at the Cheyenne center went on recreational outings to various locations in the area. They enjoyed such activities as horseback riding and skiing.

Kitagawa began her service with United Air Lines as the company was celebrating the thirtieth anniversary of the stewardess profession pioneered by the company. "I always wanted to be a stewardess," she said. "I remember how much I enjoyed the flights I had taken on airlines that served the Islands."[106]

PEGGY VERMILYEA

Peggy Vermilyea did not have to travel far from her residence in Wheatland, Wyoming, to attend the stewardess training school in Cheyenne. She finally joined her classmates in November 1960, after the seventy-five-mile drive south from her hometown.

The petite young woman was nearly too short to meet the strict requirements for becoming a stewardess. On her first try, she was turned down because her legs were "too thick." After a diet and exercise regimen,

Peggy Vermilyea (*seated in the front row, far right*) graduated from the United Air Lines Cheyenne Stewardess School on November 3, 1960. *Courtesy of Barbara Loftus.*

she was accepted. She wanted to become a stewardess to see the country and have experiences beyond those available in her small town.

One of Vermilyea's indelible memories from training, according to her daughter Barbara Loftus, was going through decompression training. Peggy told her daughter how her plane flew to a certain altitude and the instructors decompressed the plane. She experienced the effect of the sudden change in pressure as loss of coordination, and a sense of being much more able than one actually is, and then loss of consciousness.

Peggy Vermilyea and her classmates graduated on November 3, 1960, and several were assigned to Midway Airport in Chicago. She received her first paycheck for $116 on December 1, 1960.

The glamourous lifestyle stereotypical of the stewardess life during the 1960s was very much enjoyed by Vermilyea, according to her brief diary entries. She accepted many invitations to attend dinners, museums, nightclubs and other outings during her stewardess service. Her route took her to the cities of Denver, Boston, Des Moines, Los Angeles, Toledo, Newark, Baltimore, Seattle, Lincoln and Phoenix.

A few of the young woman's interesting flights included working on a chartered flight taking the Green Bay Packers to Detroit on November 23 and 24, 1960, and a charter flight with the Chicago Cubs on May 29, 1961.

The romantic life of flying ended for Vermilyea when she married engineer Gary Loftus on March 11, 1962. They lived in Chicago, Louisiana, North Carolina and South Carolina. Peggy Vermilyea Loftus moved back to Wheatland, Wyoming, in 1997 and died there in 2008.

"I have often thought how brave my mom was to have gone to stewardess school and moved from Wheatland, Wyoming, to Chicago to be all on her own at age twenty," said her daughter, Barbara Loftus. "What a different life it was as a stewardess based in Chicago compared to life as a farm girl in Wheatland."[107]

Farewell to an Era

After thirty-four years of aviation association between United Air Lines and the city of Cheyenne, Wyoming, the education and training center closed in November 1961. In addition to the stewardess training facility, the management and field training centers were also moved to new headquarters in Chicago.

Boeing Air Transport, a United Air Lines predecessor, inaugurated air service on July 1, 1927, serving Cheyenne on its route between San Francisco and Chicago. In 1930, Boeing Air Transport hired the world's first eight stewardesses.

As stewardesses stepped onto their first flights in 1930 out of Cheyenne's airport, they were joining a long and glorious history of transportation that this small town on the high plains enjoyed. Prior to the town's establishment in 1867, the trip across the continent was arduous. In 1830, it took six months for covered wagons to travel from Missouri to the Pacific coast. By 1856, the route required twenty-one days by stagecoach. Trains were the next great venture in destroying space and time across the continent. The builders of the Union Pacific Railroad had sought the easiest grade to pass through the Rocky Mountains and found that path through southern Wyoming. The route was chosen because it formed a nearly straight line between Omaha and San Francisco. Cheyenne, Wyoming, was a major station on the railroad's route and was located at the foot of the lowest point across the Continental Divide at 8,200 feet. Because of its magnificent geographic location, Cheyenne's destiny as the nation's gateway through the Rockies was secure. It sat on a route that would reduce the time to cross the nation to only seven days.[108]

Fate had placed the young city in exactly the right location to host two other great modes of transportation: the Lincoln Highway, the world's first transcontinental automobile route in 1913; and the U.S. Air Mail route, the first of its kind the world had seen. The United States Post Office began the first coast-to-coast airmail service on September 8, 1920. The airmail planes mostly followed the tracks of the railroad from Chicago to San Francisco, taking seventy hours. The first mail was flown only in daylight hours, with trains carrying the mail at night. When the idea for a transcontinental airmail route was conceived, Cheyenne was considered as a natural division point for the airmail service for the same reasons that were deemed desirable by the builders of the railroad. The speed of transit by air had annihilated yet more time from the trip across America.[109]

In order to spur progress of air transport in the country, Congress passed the Kelly Act in 1925. This act stipulated the airmail service was to be contracted to commercial air carriers. In January 1927, Boeing Air Transport won the contract for the western sector between Chicago and San Francisco and began flying mail and passengers. To facilitate the operations of this new airline, Boeing Air Transport established its headquarters in Cheyenne. In addition to guiding the operations of what was quickly becoming the largest airline in the country, the city was also home for the airline's primary maintenance base responsible for keeping the growing fleet of aircraft sky worthy. Hundreds of employees worked on all aspects of the craft and

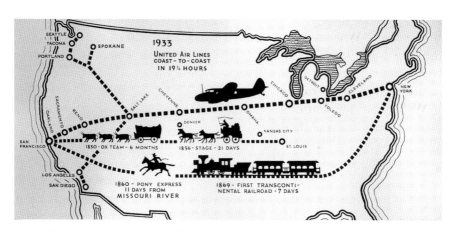

A map shows the route of the Mainliner plane as it traveled nearly the same route as earlier modes of transportation. *United Air Lines.*

became extremely adept at their tasks. By 1930, Boeing Air Transport was operating one of the largest airline aviation facilities in the world out of a small community of barely twelve thousand people.[110]

The benefits of utilizing the new air service were bountiful for passengers, too. Boeing Air Transport flew the route between San Francisco and Chicago on July 1, 1927. Passengers paid $400 for a flight that took thirty-two hours and required thirteen refueling stops en route. These early flights were often bumpy and uncomfortable, but the speed of transit across the countryside was incomparable. By 1929, Boeing's trimotor planes had cut the journey to only twenty-eight hours and reduced the fare to $260. Conditions for the air traveler began to improve when Boeing hired the world's first stewardesses to provide in-flight service for passengers.[111]

From the beginning, Cheyenne was linked with the stewardess profession since the candidates' first domicile was Cheyenne. Steve Stimpson, Boeing manager in San Francisco, and Ellen Church, a registered nurse and chief stewardess, conducted the first course for stewardesses in Cheyenne in May 1930.

Thereafter, stewardess training was conducted rather informally, often with new candidates being taught by those who had preceded them. United Air Lines opened a formal training school in Chicago in 1936.

During World War II, the Cheyenne airfield was kept humming with the war effort when thousands of workers arrived in the city to help with modification of airplanes at the Modification Number 10 facility. The now legendary capacity of United's aircraft maintenance crews at Cheyenne turned out a staggering 5,736 B-17 bombers, or 47 percent of that legendary type of aircraft used during the conflict in a span of only a little less than three years.[112] When the production line of the B-17 closed in late July 1945, the citizens of Cheyenne thought they had little to fear. United was still doing well, and there was high hope that peace would bring additional prosperity to the city. Fate had a different future in mind.

With the conclusion of the war, United Air Lines was presented with a dilemma. Cheyenne had been its maintenance base since 1927. The war, however, had provided the company with an opportunity. In the San Francisco Bay area, United had run another modification center. Instead of bombers, this facility took care of the brand-new C-54 Skymaster plane. This remarkable plane was designed specifically to fly across the vast distances of the Pacific Ocean to Australia and beyond. It boasted a pressurized cabin, powerful engines and a phenomenal range. With the conclusion of the war, the government sought to divest itself of hundreds of the aircraft with the expectation that they would be converted into modern airliners. United determined that having the maintenance base in California allowed the airline to keep up with this new age of flight.[113]

Cheyenne was relegated to secondary importance with these developments. Its base was designed to handle older aircraft that were soon going to be phased out of service. In addition, services that were provided at the small-town airfield would be better placed in major metropolitan areas now that its geographic location was no longer a dominating factor. Discussions began in 1947 to discontinue United's maintenance facilities in Cheyenne, and it seemed that the city's connection to the airways was over. Fortunately, William Patterson, the president of United, refused to abandon the loyal community altogether. Instead he ordered that a new stewardess school, desperately needed with anticipated growth of the industry then apparent, would be located at Cheyenne for the foreseeable future. The stewardess school was moved from Chicago to Cheyenne in 1947 and remained there for fourteen years.

Approximately 6,700 stewardesses received training at the Cheyenne center. Additionally, about 10,000 personnel received education in management or field training at the Wyoming school. Stewardesses attended classes for five weeks, and management and field personnel attended one-week developmental courses. Field training included courses to develop and produce aids for on-the-job, supplementary and preparatory field instruction for ground, public contact and service employees.

One aspect that required so many stewardesses to be trained during this time was retention. The consequence of a stewardess having to remain unmarried was that the average tenure for her working time was eighteen to twenty-four months, particularly in the immediate postwar era. When she left the service for marriage, a stewardess gave up her "wings," and thus the term "clipped wings" was coined. One woman who had to step aside during this time for exactly that reason was Jackie Jos Ceaser. In 1941, she formed the United Air Lines Clipped Wings group in Chicago so that former attendants had a link with friends and the airline. The group was a social club in the beginning but later became active in philanthropy. During World War II, it assisted the Red Cross. Dozens of chapters throughout the country continue to support the group's causes, such as involvement with Special Olympics.[114]

There was constant change from the time the first stewardesses arrived in Cheyenne for training in 1930 until the last class graduated in 1961. Stewardess unions were formed in 1946, supporting improved wages and

This 1962 photo shows (*left to right*) Mary O'Connor, longtime UAL employee; Steve Stimpson, originator of the idea for women stewardesses; Ellen Church, world's first airline stewardess; and Jackie Jos Ceaser, founder of United Air Lines Clipped Wings. *United Air Lines.*

working conditions. United Air Lines hired eight Hawaiian men to serve on its route between the mainland and Hawaii in 1950. The men could marry and have families, whereas the stewardesses still had to remain single.[115]

An unusual event occurred at the stewardess training school in Cheyenne when four airmen attended classes for five weeks in September 1949. The four men came from Hickam Air Force Base in Hawaii and were on duty as Military Air Transport Service (MATS) flight attendants. On September 23, 1949, F.E. Warren Air Force Base's newspaper, the *Warren Mustang*, said, "This school will make them more efficient at their duties as Flight Attendants for MATS."[116]

With the arrival of the jet age in 1958, things began to change for the stewardesses as well as for the Cheyenne training school. The school integrated new technology into the training program. Along with new emergency procedures, training was modified to deal with the new technology of the DC-8 and the subsequent reduction of flight time with larger numbers of passengers. Instructors could be frequently seen coaxing and nudging trainees down the new inflatable slides suspended nearly ten feet off the ground. Along with slide training, the stewardesses had to contend with automatic drop-down oxygen masks, more efficient galleys for food service, trays attached to seat backs, the service of liquor on board the aircraft, in-flight movies and the growing use of computerization.[117]

The Civil Rights Act of 1964 prohibited discrimination on the basis of age, sex, race and marital status. The act also brought about a revision of job training and requirements. The airlines adopted the new name of flight attendant and accepted men and women for jobs the female stewardesses had formerly held.

Time, it would seem, had caught up with the airlines in general and the city of Cheyenne in particular. New technology and management decisions ultimately caused the decline of Cheyenne's glorious air age.

The United Air Lines' education and training center was moved to a $2 million building adjacent to the new executive headquarters near O'Hare International Airport. This facility, known as Jet Age University, took over the stewardess training program that had been in Cheyenne for fourteen years. Instead of open dormitories and jury-built classrooms, the new facility offered dedicated classrooms, dormitory suites, a cafeteria, a year-round swimming pool, tennis courts, a full plane mockup and beauty salons.[118]

Graduation of Cheyenne's final two classes of stewardesses occurred on November 3, 1961, with forty-one students receiving diplomas at ceremonies in Denver, Colorado. The move to Chicago also meant that staff responsible for stewardess, management and field training would be transferred to the new facility. Superintendents transferring to Chicago included T.B. Wardell, stewardess training; Jack Hayes, management training; and J.J. Heavey, field training.[119]

The November 2, 1961 edition of the *Wyoming Eagle* lamented that aside from the loss of the economic benefits of the stewardess school, the city also lost a romantic connection to a time when ladies of the sky visited the Wigwam Lounge in the Plains Hotel. The town and its airfield became quieter in 1961 with the loss of the school, and several people yearned for the time when Wyoming gave the ambassadors of the "Friendly Skies" their wings.[120]

In the ensuing years, the Cheyenne airfield continued to decline in terms of passenger service, with only brief upticks in activity. The airfield has since become a home to a number of aviation enterprises of various sizes.

The major tenant of the Cheyenne airfield remains the Wyoming Air National Guard. When the stewardess school was in operation, the National Guard occupied the hangar and facilities connected to the school building. Unverified verbal accounts stated that if any members of the guard strayed over to the stewardess side of the facility, there would be severe consequences. However, former stewardess Patty Seibel Romeo, who attended the Cheyenne

Pat Sloan of Louisville (*center left*) and Ann Dempsey of Seattle (*center right*) celebrated their birthdays in June 1958 with other trainee friends at the Wigwam Lounge in the Plains Hotel, Cheyenne, a favorite stewardess meeting place at the time. *Wyoming State Archives, Department of State Parks and Cultural Resources.*

school, said stewardesses and members of the military did meet and go on dates. Some stewardesses and military men from Cheyenne eventually married as well.[121]

The other use of the airfield is as home to a myriad of corporate, private and state aircraft and as a stopover by general aviation enthusiasts. From time to time, major aircraft companies have attempted to use Cheyenne as a hub for commuter air services, but most of these have faded away.

To many, Cheyenne's great aviation heritage has dimmed to a vague memory. Surrounded on all sides by neighborhoods and shopping districts, the airfield often gets derision as being badly placed right in the middle of a city that was in fact allowed to grow around it. Activities at the Cheyenne Airport sometimes startle citizens, as huge aircraft pay it a visit from the military. Sometimes aircraft from Denver are diverted to Cheyenne in times of bad weather delays. Boeing Aircraft Corporation also frequently tests its newest aircraft at the airfield for landing and crosswind performance tests.

The Wyoming National Guard hangar was located next to the United Air Lines Stewardess Training Center in Cheyenne, Wyoming. *Michael Kassel photo.*

The new terminal built in 2018 at the Cheyenne, Wyoming airport. *Starley Talbott photo.*

The original eight stewardesses posed for a photograph in the reception area of the Cheyenne, Wyoming airport terminal following training in May 1930, before launching a new career for women in flight. *United Air Lines.*

As time goes by, many of Cheyenne's citizens remember the romantic era when passenger planes landed more frequently in the city. Some folks still long for the days when dazzling young women from around the country came to learn and play in this windy high-plains city.

Cheyenne maintains hope that the glory of its aviation past will return. In 2018, the city completed a brand-new $18 million airport terminal. The former airport terminal had become too small and functionally obsolete to accommodate modern travel requirements. The new twenty-eight-thousand-square-foot state-of-the-art terminal accommodates rental car services and offers complimentary parking and other passenger amenities. Cheyenne was recognized as the fastest-growing small airport in the nation in 2019.[122]

It remains to be seen whether or not new tidings of great things will land once again in Cheyenne. The citizens hold lofty hopes and dreams, along with sky-high ideas, just like the original eight stewardesses did ninety years ago.

Notes

Chapter 1

1. Stimpson, "Reminiscing."
2. Kassel, "United Airlines Stewardess School," 11–18.
3. Garvey and Fisher, *Age of Flight*, 76.
4. Stimpson, "Reminiscing."
5. Ibid.
6. United Air Lines [hereafter UAL] News Bureau, October 1947.
7. UAL Archives.
8. Ibid.
9. Taylor, *"Pat" Patterson*, 36.
10. Stimpson, "Reminiscing."
11. Mahler, *Legacy*, 68.
12. Kassel, "United Airlines Stewardess School," 11–18.
13. Stimpson, "Reminiscing."
14. Kassel, "United Airlines Stewardess School," 11–18.
15. UAL Archives historical document.
16. *Wyoming Tribune*, May 14, 1930.
17. Stimpson, *Boeing Original Stewardess Manual*.
18. Ibid.
19. Ibid.
20. Ibid.
21. Ibid.
22. Ibid.

23. Ibid.

24. Ibid.

25. Stimpson, "Reminiscing."

26. McLaughlin, *Footsteps in the Sky*, 19.

27. Stimpson, "Reminiscing."

28. Ibid.

29. *Boeing News*, October 10, 1930, 6.

30. Ibid., December 1930, 4.

31. *United Air Lines News*, March 1933.

Chapter 2

32. *Boeing System Revised Stewardess Manual,* January 15, 1931.

33. *Boeing System Revised Stewardess Manual,* January 1, 1933.

34. Ibid.

35. Garvey and Fisher, *Age of Flight*, 97–100.

36. UAL, news brief.

37. Garvey and Fisher, *Age of Flight*, 136.

38. UAL, news brief.

39. Larson, *History of Wyoming*, 490.

40. Garvey and Fisher, *Age of Flight*, 196.

41. UAL News Bureau.

42. Kassel, *Annals of Wyoming*.

Chapter 3

43. Ibid.

44. *Wyoming State Tribune*, April 4, 1946.

45. Hayes, interview.

46. UAL, news notes.

47. UAL newsletter, November 1948.

48. UAL newsletter, February 1950.

49. Hayes, interview.

50. *United Air Lines Stewardess Manual,* January 28, 1947.

51. Ibid.

52. Ibid.

53. Garvey and Fisher, *Age of Flight*, 133.

54. Ibid.

55. Ibid.
56. Ibid., 136.
57. McLaughlin, *Footsteps in the Sky*, 225.
58. Garvey and Fisher, *Age of Flight*, 150.
59. McLaughlin, *Footsteps in the Sky*, 98.
60. *United Air Lines Stewardess Manual*, 1947.
61. McLaughlin, *Footsteps in the Sky*, 100.
62. UAL Stewardess Management Conference, September 11–13, 1951.
63. Ibid.
64. UAL, news brief, June 1950.
65. Ibid.
66. UAL Report, 1957.

Chapter 4

67. UAL News Bureau, September 1, 1959
68. Ibid.
69. Radio interview, April 16, 1945.
70. First Allied Airborne Army Public Relations Office, news release to United Air Lines, September 1944.
71. UAL News Bureau, September 1, 1959.
72. Radio interview, April 16, 1945.
73. UAL News Bureau, September 1, 1959.
74. UAL News Bureau, luncheon ceremony, 1966.
75. Associated Press, "Harriet and Her Little Green Swallows Flew the Unfriendly Skies," May 1970.
76. Stimpson, "Reminiscing."
77. McLaughlin, *Footsteps in the Sky*, 16–18.
78. Ibid.
79. Chicago News Bureau, May 1950.
80. McLaughlin, *Footsteps in the Sky*, 18.
81. UAL News Bureau, 50th Anniversary of Stewardess Service, 1980.
82. Ibid.
83. Ibid.
84. Ibid.
85. Ibid.
86. McLaughlin, *Footsteps in the Sky*, 19.
87. Ibid.

88. UAL, news briefs.

89. Mahler, *Legacy*, 60.

90. McLaughlin, *Footsteps in the Sky*, 19.

91. Ibid.

92. UAL, news briefs.

93. Ibid.

94. McLaughlin, *Footsteps in the Sky*, 24.

95. Ibid.

96. Garvey and Fisher, *Age of Flight*, 62–63.

97. UAL, news briefs.

98. Ibid.

Chapter 5

99. Fitzpatrick, interview.

100. Forbes, interview.

101. Dittman to Forbes letter, April 17, 2003.

102. Telephone interview with authors Talbott and Kassel, 2019.

103. Romeo and Romeo, interview.

104. Jack, interview.

105. UAL News Bureau.

106. UAL News Bureau, 1960.

107. Loftus, email correspondence.

Chapter 6

108. Talbott and Kassel, *Wyoming Airmail Pioneers*, 11–12.

109. Ibid.

110. Ibid.

111. Garvey and Fisher, *Age of Flight*, 73.

112. Ibid., 196.

113. "UAL to Expand on West Coast: Repair Facilities Will Be Centered in San Francisco," *Wyoming State Tribune*, April 4, 1946, 1, 11.

114. McLaughlin, *Footsteps in the Sky*, 313.

115. Garvey and Fisher, *Age of Flight*, 63.

116. "Four Airmen to Attend Stewardess School in Cheyenne," *Warren Mustang*, September 23, 1949, 3.

117. Mahler, *Legacy*, 124, 134.
118. Ibid., 141.
119. UAL News Bureau, November 1961.
120. *Wyoming Eagle*, November 2, 1961.
121. Romeo, interview.
122. Volk, "Cheyenne Marks 1 Year."

Bibliography

Fitzpatrick, Mildred Sturdevant. Personal interview, February 20, 2020.

Forbes, Jane. Interview with Michael Kassel, April 13 and 21, 2003

Garvey, William, and David Fisher. *The Age of Flight*. Greensboro, NC: Pace Communications, 2002.

Haring, David. *Cheyenne Airport 2000 Economic Impact Study*. Cheyenne, WY, January 2002.

Hayes, Jack. Interview with Michael Kassel, April 15, 2003.

Jack, Phyllis. Personal interview, February 20, 2020.

Kassel, Michael. "The United Airlines Stewardess School in Cheyenne, Wyoming." *Annals of Wyoming* 75, no. 4 (Autumn 2003): 11–18.

Larson, T.A. *History of Wyoming*. Lincoln: University of Nebraska Press, 1978.

Loftus, Barbara. Email communications with the authors, January 11–14, 2020.

Mahler, Gwen. *Legacy of the Friendly Skies*. Marceline, MO: Walsworth Publishing Company, 1991.

McAllister, Bruce, and Stephan Wilkinson. *Skygirls*. Boulder, CO: Roundup Press, 2012.

McLaughlin, Helen. *Footsteps in the Sky*. Denver, CO: State of the Art Ltd., 1994.

Romeo, Patricia Seibel, and Tony Romeo. Personal interview, September 21, 2019.

Stewart, Alda Kessler. Interview with the authors, September 2019.

Stimpson, Steve. *Boeing Original Stewardess Manual.* May 1, 1930. United Air Lines Archives, Chicago.

———. *Boeing System Revised Stewardess Manual.* January 15, 1931. United Air Lines Archives, Chicago.

———. "Reminiscing." United Air Lines 25th Anniversary Luncheon, May 22, 1955. United Air Lines Archives, Chicago.

Talbott, Starley, and Michael E. Kassel. *Wyoming Airmail Pioneers.* Charleston, SC: The History Press, 2017.

Taylor, Frank J. *"Pat" Patterson.* Menlo Park, CA: Lane Magazine & Book Company, 1967.

United Air Lines News Bureau and News Briefs, from United Air Lines Archives, accessed by authors October 15, 2019.

Volk, Wendy. "Cheyenne Marks 1 Year of Record-Breaking Air Service." *Wyoming Tribune Eagle,* October 31, 2019.

Warren Mustang. "Four Airmen to Attend Stewardess School in Cheyenne." September 23, 1949.

Wyoming Eagle. "Loss of Stewardess School." November 2, 1961.

Wyoming State Tribune. "UAL to Expand on West Coast: Repair Facilities Will Be Centered in San Francisco." April 4, 1946.

Wyoming Tribune. "Eight Nurses Land Here to Serve on Transport Planes." May 14, 1930.

———. "United Announces Relocation of Stewardess School." April 4, 1946.

———. "United Stewardess Service Celebrates 31st Anniversary." July 25, 1961.

Wyoming Tribune Eagle. "It Started in Cheyenne 40 Years Ago." May 24, 1970.

Websites

WyoHistory.org, A Project of the Wyoming State Historical Society. wyohistory.org.

Wyoming Newspapers, From the Wyoming State Library. newspapers.wyo. gov.

Wyoming State Archives. wyoarchives.state.wy.

About the Authors

STARLEY TALBOTT has been a freelance author for more than forty years. She has been published in numerous newspapers and magazines throughout the Rocky Mountain region and is the author of eight books, including three Arcadia Publishing titles: *Platte County*, *Fort Laramie* and *Cheyenne Frontier Days*; and two History Press titles: *Wyoming Airmail Pioneers* and *A History of the Wyoming Capitol*. Starley holds a BS degree from the University of Wyoming and an MS degree from the University of Nevada. She has lived in several states and foreign countries, loves to travel and has a deep appreciation for history. She is a member of Wyoming Writers, Platte County Historical Society and the Wyoming State Historical Society.

MICHAEL E. KASSEL serves as the curator of collections and is the co-director of the Cheyenne Frontier Days Old West Museum. He is an adjunct professor of history at Laramie County Community College in Cheyenne, Wyoming. He holds a BS degree in historic preservation from Southeast Missouri State University, an Associate of the Arts degree in history from Laramie County Community College and a Master of Arts degree from the University of Wyoming. He is the author of *Thunder on High: Cheyenne, Denver and Aviation Supremacy on the Rocky Mountain Front Range* and "The United Air Lines Stewardess School in Cheyenne, Wyoming." He is the coauthor of *Wyoming Air Mail Pioneers* from The History Press.

Visit us at
www.historypress.com
······································